Primary English in the National Curriculum

List of Contributors

Contact with contributors may be facilitated through UKRA Administrative Office, Edgehill College of Education, St Helen's Road, Ormskirk, Lancs. L39 4QP

Christine Anderson, former teacher and past President of UKRA; 10 Hallhead Road, Edinburgh RH16 5QJ

Ronald Arnold, Adviser for English and Language Development, Oxfordshire LEA, Visiting Professor of Education, Kingston Polytechnic, London, former HMI and secretary to the Bullock Committee; Education Department, Macclesfield House, New Road, Oxford OX1 1NA

John Bald, Tutor in Charge, Essex County Language and Reading Centre; Curriculum Development Centre, Acaria Avenue, Colchester CO4 3TQ

Roger Beard, Senior Lecturer in Primary Education and editor of UKRA monograph series; School of Education, University of Leeds, Leeds LS2 9JT

Sue Beverton, Senior Lecturer, Special Educational Needs and convener of UKRA Research Committee; Faculty of In-service Education, Communications and Computing, New College, Neville's Cross Centre, Darlington Road, Durham

Richard Binns, Lecturer, Special Educational Needs, affiliated to St Andrews College of Education; 17 Montrose Gardens, Milagane, Glasgow G62 8NQ

Peter Brinton, Deputy Headteacher and convener of UKRA Publications Committee; 11 St George's Road, Truro, Cornwall TR1 3JE

Ken Byron, Teacher–Adviser for Drama; Knighton Fields Teachers' Centre, Herrick Road, Leicester LE6 2DJ

Doug Dennis, Director of Studies, past President of UKRA and convener of UKRA Teacher Education Committee; Worcester College of Higher Education, Henwich Grove, Worcester WR2 6HA

Alan Dyson, Lecturer, Special Educational Needs, School of Education, University of Newcastle, Newcastle-upon-Tyne

Keith Gardner, consultant and past President of UKRA, 45 South Hermitage Street, Newcastleton TD9 0QE

Peter Garrett, Lecturer; School of English and Linguistics, University College of North Wales, Bangor, Gwynedd LL57 2DG

W. A. Gatherer, consultant and former Chief Adviser, Lothian Region; 44 Liberton Drive, Edinburgh EH16 6NN

Kay Goodall, Lecturer in Primary Education; Keele University, Keele, Staffs.

Colin Harrison, Senior Lecturer and past President of UKRA; School of Education, University Park, Nottingham NG7 2RD

Morag Hunter-Carsch, Lecturer in Education and past President of UKRA, School of Education, University of Leicester, 21 University Road, Leicester LE1 7RF

Carl James, Senior Lecturer and Acting Head of Section; School of English and Linguistics, University College of North Wales, Bangor, Gwynedd LL57 2DG

Margaret Litchfield, Area Head; Area 1, Literacy Support Service, Knighton Fields Teachers' Centre, Herrick Road, Leicester LE6 2DJ

Alison B. Littlefair, consultant; 56 High Street, Harlton, Cambridge CB3 7ES

Joyce Morris, consultant, writer, founder member and past President of UKRA; 33 Deena Close, Queens Drive, London W3 OHR

David Moseley, Reader in Applied Psychology; 259 Wingrove Road, Fenham, Newcastle-upon-Tyne NE4 9OD

Cecilia Obrist, writer and consultant; Denbigh House, Woodside, Aspley Guise, Milton Keynes

Sue Palmer, writer and teacher; 11 St George's Road, Truro, Cornwall TR1 3JE

Anne Stuart, researcher and former Lecturer at Manchester Polytechnic; 11a Astley Grove, Stalybridge, Cheshire SK15 1NL

Sarah Tann, Reader; School of Education, Oxford Polytechnic, Wheatley, Oxford OX9 1HX

Christopher Winch, Senior Lecturer in Reading and Language Development; Faculty of Education and Social Science, Park Campus, Nene College, Northampton

George Young, consultant; 7 Windsor Close, Oadby, Leicester

Primary English in the National Curriculum

Edited by Morag Hunter-Carsch,
Sue Beverton and Doug Dennis

Blackwell Education

First published 1990

Basil Blackwell Ltd
108 Cowley Road
Oxford OX4 1JF
UK

British Library Cataloguing in Publication Data
Primary English in the National curriculum.
  1. Great Britain. Primary schools. Curriculum subjects: English language. Teaching
  I. Hunter–Carsch, Morag II. Beverton, Sue III. Dennis, Douglas
  372.6′044′0941

ISBN 0–631–17319–6
ISBN 0–631–90482–4 pbk

Typeset in 11 on 13 point Plantin by
Photo·graphics, Honiton, Devon
Printed and bound in Great Britain by TJ Press Ltd, Cornwall

Contents

Foreword

Every time the British educational world is subjected to cataclysmic changes of direction the subject of English lies at the heart of national debate. Perhaps more than any other thing taught, English is frequently subjected to carpings and criticisms, and less frequently to constructive review and analysis. Its central place in the curriculum makes it inevitable that it should be the focus of attention, and it is gratifying to those of us who have invested so much of ourselves in its development that it should be brought again to the forefront of political and educational change. The government's anxiety that English teaching should be improved is to be welcomed, and the appearance of the studies, reports and guidelines which form the subject of this book emphasises the social and cultural importance of Primary English.

There are some important reasons, however, why the public demand for changes in English teaching must be accompanied by informed professional discussion. One is, quite simply, that the English skills of our pupils are never good enough. Everyone who requires English of a certain standard, whether in speech or writing, or for understanding or communication or self-expression, is constantly reminded of the elusive nature of language and the virtual impossibility of achieving exactly the language wanted. However effective our teaching may be, it will always need to be better. But many who are aware of the difficultness of using language to perfection remain sadly unconscious of the difficultness of teaching pupils to use it well. Lay persons can be forgiven for expecting more of our pupils than those of us who are professional teachers are able to deliver. We would wish them, however, to know more about English as a school discipline and how it is learned and taught, if only so that they might appreciate more sensitively what are our problems and needs as teachers. It is a good reason for welcoming this book that it provides such detailed and lucid accounts of 'what language is and does as well as how best to teach it', as the editors neatly put it.

Another reason why English is always at the centre of any educational storm is that we are never all agreed what should be taught in its name. I well remember, as an HMI, meeting a little girl who said that she 'hated English'. It turned out that she loved reading and poetry and drama and writing stories, but hated 'English', which she perceived as slot-filling exercises and parsing words and grammatical analysis. She could make no mental connection between even the useful vocabulary-building exercises and her own creative strivings to produce the language she wanted to enjoy. It is worrying to reflect that neither could her teachers; nor can many a present-day politician or journalist. Whether or not there *are* genuine connections is not the real question. The important question is whether people realise *why* teachers do what they do in their efforts to teach English. The contributors to this book set out to discuss questions about what should be taught as English, and why, and how it can best be done: but they are too professionally wise to be caught providing facile answers. English teachers suffer more than most from know-all lay persons who think they know what pupils need – more grammar, more spelling, less frills and so on. What the popular newspapers call a 'massive shake-up' in the teaching of English cannot be accomplished at that shallow level of awareness. The writers of this book would wish to be seen helping teachers to understand the deep and complex questions about English and to come by themselves to a better knowledge of the tentative solutions which we call methods, approaches, techniques. It is to be hoped that the book will also help teachers to cope with ill-informed public critics who would divert them from the best-tried ways of teaching.

It has been a very special pleasure for me to read the papers in this book and to be given the privilege of writing this foreword. It is not only that I have spent a long career in the field of English teaching – not only that it fell to my good fortune to become UKRA's first Honorary Life Member – it is, above all, that this gives me the opportunity of commending to all who are interested in children and teaching another outstanding example of the Association's work.

W.A. GATHERER

Part I
Contextual Concerns

Introduction

This introduction provides a rationale for the organisation of the various contributing chapters to this book under four headings:

I   Contextual Concerns
II The Kingman Channel
III The Wider Bullock Way: Cox and Beyond
IV The Ocean of Literacy

Such a sequence of sections metaphorically flows from the National Curriculum outwards, anticipating the international concern for literacy which is symbolised in the challenge and celebration implicit in Unesco's citing of 1990 as International Literacy Year.

Part I, Contextual Concerns, begins in Chapter 1 with a discussion of the aims of this book. The kind of communication which is envisaged would need to take into account what we already know. Thus Chapters 2 and 3 address issues of continuity as well as change, endorsing the wisdom of the educator, Christian Schiller, who said: 'We cannot predict the future – we can, if we will, influence the movement of change and sometimes even guide it. But we must have clearly in our minds a direction in which we want to go: we cannot know the path . . . we need a star, a distant star, a vision that's the sort of direction we want to follow when we can' (Griffin-Beale 1979).

The 'kind of vision' can become clouded by conceptual confusion, false polarisations and distractions which, like presences in the mist, can loom larger than life. One such area of potential confusion and distraction is that of grammar and its place in the curriculum. Chapter 4 takes a look directly at this issue which is further discussed in various chapters in Parts II and III.

The whole question of values and realities underpins the wider debate on the above issues, requiring us to look closely at what language is and does as well as how best to teach it. Thus Chapter 5 explores what was said about the findings of the Committee of Inquiry into the Teaching of English Language, as reported in the newspapers. Chapter 6 looks at what the Chairman of the Committee, Sir John Kingman, actually said in a guest lecture on the Report. Theoretical aspects of the Report are discussed in Chapters 7 and 8 while Chapter 9 considers some practical implications. The issue of what exactly we mean when we use the term 'language awareness' is taken up in Chapter 10 for which we are indebted to the organisers of the British Association for Applied Linguistics Conference of that title in March 1989 in Bangor.

One of the ways of avoiding false antitheses, Whitehead (1967) suggested, is to take into account the 'Rhythm of Education' which can provide sufficient motivation for learners to be carried through all three stages in this principle of education: first, the stage of 'Romance' in which the learner is involved in the experience as a whole; secondly, the stage of 'Precision' in which study of detail is required; and thirdly, the stage of 'Generalisation' in which the learning can be put to use. The problem which Whitehead pointed towards is that of introducing ideas which both begin and end at stage two. Such ideas he referred to as 'inert ideas'. Thus we see the difficulty posed by ideas about the teaching of grammar. They need to be introduced in such a way as to motivate the learner or maintain the learner's already established motivation to communicate. Thus learning 'what' and 'how' should complement the existing interest in 'why'.

Part III begins with Chapter 11 which develops some of the conceptual and practical issues which teachers must become familiar with if they are to discuss and deal with the classroom implications of both the Kingman and Cox Reports in a way which, like Whitehead's 'Stage of Precision', engages more deeply with the details. Chapter 12 explains some of the problems which face beginner readers and writers who are involved in the task of not only decoding words in context which may help towards their recognition, but of acquiring a way of dealing with phoneme–grapheme correspondence in English. This must become so efficient that it is virtually 'automatic' to permit the reader or writer to concentrate on meaning. This kind of mastery is no small task since traditional orthography, the alphabet, does not represent sets of exclusively one to one correspondences between letters and 'sounds'. The issue is thus not so much the question of which method or methods of teaching to use as the extent to which teachers are aware of the nature of the difficulty which this system poses for some children. This in turn highlights the need for appropriate assistance at those points where there are choices to be made and the reasoning 'rules' may be less than clearly evident to the learner. Perhaps it is here that the greatest professional challenge lies, when the approach used for most of the children (or adults) does not seem to be satisfactory for all and may, in fact, reveal fairly extensive individual differences in the pacing of learning how to read and write. Should any explanations be offered? If so, how much, and in what mode (direct 'teaching'? by class or group? supported or individualised learning?)?

Chapter 13 relates the inspiration and achievements of literature to the larger challenge of developing a kind of literacy that includes a lasting love of literature throughout life. This theme is developed through Chapter 14 with its focus on poetry and Chapter 15 on drama. Together these chapters relate individual and social developmental factors. The voice and voices are needed for participation in the kind of democracy which is considered as desirable by the writers of both the Cox and Kingman Reports. In that context it becomes clear that the teacher needs to organise for the development of talk (Chapter 16) and of reading and writing for a range of purposes (Chapters 17, 18 and 19).

No response to recent reports would be complete without reference to both Assessment and Special Educational Needs (Chapters 20 and 21). In the words of Schiller, 'It is important to help young children interpret what they know in thoughts they can think in words they can speak' (Griffin-Beale, 1979).

Thus Part IV takes us from the family roots of reading experience to the recent reports (Chapter 23) to the recognition that we are not alone in our struggle to make and share meaning and thus to communicate and celebrate literacy.

We would like to express, to all writers and contributors to the exchange, our appreciation and gratitude, on behalf of the Association. Many people have contributed directly and indirectly to this book. Amongst those are Maureen Hardy and Rosemary Benn, whose names we cite to represent all those too numerous to list whose loyalty, hard work and untiring energy have made it possible to deliver the submissions to the various reports and to the making of this book. For information on Scottish curricular developments, thanks to Ronald Mackay, Assistant Principal at Jordanhill College of Education, Glasgow, Dorothy Blair of Northern College, Dundee, and Alastair Hendry, formerly of Craigie College, Ayr. Thanks are also due to Carole Fitzpatrick for typing the manuscript.

The editors wish to note that no single view of any writer represents the UKRA which remains a forum of exchange of information.

References

Department of Education and Science (1988a) *Report of the Inquiry into the Teaching of English Language* (The Kingman Report). HMSO, London.

Department of Education and Science (1988b) *English for ages 5 to 11* (The Cox Report). HMSO, London.

Griffin-Beale, C. (ed.) (1979) *Christian Schiller: In His Own Words*. A & C Black, London.

Whitehead, A. (1967) *The Aims of Education*, The Free Press, Macmillan, New York.

1 Communication: UKRA's Concerns

Morag Hunter-Carsch, Sue Beverton and Doug Dennis

Introduction

So much is happening in schools in England and Wales at present as a result of the introduction of the National Curriculum that it seems as if few teachers are able to take the time to stand back and to adopt the stance of the 'reflective practitioner'. Without a sense of professional detachment which permits the checking of curriculum content and methods against the underlying aims, the burden of the details in a flood of guidelines may seem to be overwhelming.

However pressing the demands may seem to be, we would advocate taking time to look from a distance, to gain a sense of perspective and clear vision of the direction, an image of what we are trying to achieve. To assist with such a process of detaching oneself for the purpose of reflection, we hope that dipping into the chapters of this book may prove to be useful.

Our major concern is literacy – not just basic literacy but the kind of literacy that results in 'personal growth' and increasing self-esteem. This may be achieved through the development of a mastery of knowing how and where to find out whatever is needed and how to use it. We hope that this may lead to a 'dialogue' with print, a 'conversation' with writers – processes which tend to develop a clarification of both thought and feelings. This craftsmanship now includes using the tools of information technology as well as the pen.

Such literacy provides direct access to a power, a sense of self-fulfilment which is served by literature rather than serving literature. It is the entitlement or access to that power which we believe to be a critical aspect of each child's rightful expectation of his or her education. It is in this sense that we would like to explore the relationship of reading and writing, hearing and listening. This includes listening to oneself thinking as if one were the writer. Inevitably this also affects patterns of speaking which tend progressively to be the outcomes of reflection and of inner communication, synthesising and perhaps balancing thoughts and feelings.

We wonder if that is perhaps the main purpose of all the curricular activity? Are these the qualities which render the human potential unique?

We had to dig deeply into the Government's reports to find sufficiently broad aims to serve as a conceptual framework within which the whole range of aims and objectives could be encompassed. We think we found a clue implicit in Cox II (June 1989) which concerns 'education for democracy': 'A democratic society needs people who have the linguistic abilities which will enable them to discuss, evaluate and make sense of what they have been told, as well as to take effective action on the basis of their understanding . . . otherwise there can be no genuine participation but only the imposition of ideas by those who are linguistically capable'.

Cox goes on to indicate in paragraph 2.19 that 'both aspects of language development, the personal and social, contribute to giving pupils power over their own lives'. Later in the Report there is comment about developing 'a personal voice' through writing. Links with drama and reading reflectively are easily made and the idea of 'voice' whispers throughout the Report. Recognising this power which concerns words, ideas, thinking and communicating would seem to be a prerequisite for dealing with abstract ideas, the basis for ethics and consideration of such fundamental issues as the possibility of altruism. Without such considerations our curriculum would surely fail to provide children with the means of confronting some of the central problems of survival in society and caring about others. Moral education is intimately bound up with such awareness and must be linked with the development of reason.

The informed citizens of our democracy would need to be encouraged, through their education, to recognise false dichotomies, to grasp relationships which may not be immediately apparent (a basically scientific and mathematical as well as artistic notion), and to appreciate through listening, what each perception is about (aesthetics, music and design). They would thus be able to avoid the sorts of problems which beset our current discussions of the National Curriculum when ill-informed attempts are made to polarise approaches to teaching which are caricatured by selective reference, for example, to either linguistics or literature. The teachers of English require to be well informed in both areas and all teachers may require a sufficient metalinguistic awareness to be able to deal efficiently with conceptual as well as formal problems that their pupils face in the course of developing competence in literacy across the curriculum.

While this book was planned mainly for primary teachers it may be of interest and use to secondary school teachers of a variety of subject areas, and to others.

The rationale for inclusion of the various chapters is provided in the introductory notes to each of the sections of the book. The sections relate first to the context in which the National Curriculum is being developed in England and Wales, secondly to the philosophical and linguistic underpinning of the Kingman Report's contribution to English in the curriculum, and thirdly to the implications through and beyond the Cox Reports for what, historically, is required to be a language education 'for life'. Fourthly, we report on a movement which is fostering love of literature and ways in which the UKRA membership has collectively engaged in the consultative process in the development of the National Curriculum in English. This section terminates with an invitation to consider how best to promote international literacy. This, surely, constitutes a source of concern to all of us.

The Impact of the National Curriculum

We are positive about the potential of the National Curriculum. The idea of a fair chance for all children to be offered a basic agreed curriculum is surely not in question. We celebrate the underlying principle of 'entitlement', now enshrined in law endorsing access for all children to the curriculum. The establishment of this right rings in new era for the teaching profession.

Particularly for the characteristically self-effacing primary school teachers there is the official recognition of their role as one which goes far beyond caring for young children in a holding capacity until they reach secondary schooling. They will no longer take second place as their responsibilities in the laying of the educational foundations become increasingly respected as the implications of the emphasis on continuity between primary and secondary schooling is publicly taken more seriously.

The principle of continuity which is now explicitly stated in the curriculum for ages 5–16 will undoubtedly have an impact on children's nursery education and transitions within the early years phase of education. With reference to early experience of reading, particularly through sharing books and listening to stories, poems and songs, it should become increasingly evident that the kinds of detailed guidelines provided in the Government Orders for Key Stage 1 in English may require further comment. For example, how do children acquire facility with phonological segmentation? How are reading and writing best linked in the development towards 'recognising individual words or letters in familiar contexts' (Attainment Target 2, Level 1.11)? There is still a gap between what is stated globally in the attainment targets and equally generally in the programmes of study. (See, for example, 16.22: Pupils' own writing . . . should form part of the resources . . .') More than ever before, the challenge to the profession is to make clear how educational methods relate to theoretical positions and precisely what the evidence is and continues to be in support of particular practices.

Unfortunately, however, the 1989 National Curriculum Council package, the 'Introduction to the National Curriculum' appears to be rather long on 'action' and 'assessment' and very much on the exiguous side when it comes to a delineation of aims. Consequently, those who do not turn to other documents in search of the connections, the criteria on which both action and assessment are based, are at some risk.

Nevertheless, the curricular framework is going to make the discussion of research more focused in the first instance and holds the potential for exploration beyond the basic outlines as they currently stand. Entitlement or access to the curriculum prescribes the basis or expected minimum. It does not set the upper limits. In that way there is much room at the top and more likelihood that there will be recognition in due course for the excellence of the teaching which we know exists amongst classrooms up and down the land.

There is also the likelihood that there will be an increase in professional confidence to refute arguments about alleged 'poor quality of teaching' since the assessment, monitoring and record keeping that will be required should lead to clearer professional discussion about what is meant by 'standards' and thus to what can fairly be communicated to the public on that topic through the channels of school boards with 'trained governors'. Local, regional and national discussions should be the better informed as a result of having the common ground of the curriculum guidelines. It is nevertheless to be hoped that we can raise the level of debate on the central issues concerning not only what the children learn but how they learn and why we attribute such value to their schooling. In that context it is likely that we would very quickly arrive at the recognition of the merit of the aim to develop children's thinking across the curriculum.

The relationship between thinking and literacy is explored by Margaret Donaldson in 'Sense and Sensibility: Some Thoughts on the Teaching of Literacy' (1989). She comments that 'thinking itself draws great strength from literacy – whenever it is more than just a scrap of an idea, whenever there is a discussion to develop, whenever there are complex possibilities to consider. It is even more obvious that the sustained, orderly communication of this kind of thinking requires a considerable mastery of the written word.'

Later in the same paper, Professor Donaldson develops her argument, explaining also the relationship between literacy and literature. In paying tribute to the cogency of her argument, and respectfully recommending readers to fill in the gap by turning to the full paper, we leap to her final point which provides us with the assurance that 'there is, most fortunately, no incompatibility between developing a love of literature, with all the personal enrichment which that brings, and developing the ways of handling language that favour clear, sustained rational thought. These can and should develop side by side, through the school years.'

The UKRA and the Making of this Book

This book constitutes a sharing of responses by members of the UKRA to recent events in education in England and Wales in developing the National Curriculum and particularly in the subject area of English.

The aims of the book are threefold:

1   to share and continue discussions in response to the invitation by Sir John Kingman to become involved in 'raising the level of debate about the teaching of English language';
2   to locate these discussions in the wider context of issues in the teaching of English within the curriculum as a whole;
3   to introduce some thoughts about International Literacy Year.

The manner in which we have responded is in keeping with the aims of the UKRA, which are to:

● encourage the study of reading and reading problems at all educational levels;
● stimulate and promote research in reading;
● publish the results of pertinent and significant investigations;
● assist in the development of teacher training programmes;
● act as a clearing house for information relating to reading;
● disseminate knowledge helpful in the solution of problems relating to reading and to sponsor conferences and meetings planned to implement the purposes of the Association.

Reading

The view of reading generally shared by the membership is one which recognises the broader interpretation of the process as one which is intimately connected with literacy, language, learning and communication. There is no one approach to the teaching of reading which is exclusively supported by the Association. Rather it is a forum for exchange of information on this and related issues. The assumption is that human nature is variable – that certain perspectives may be effective for some people whereas other people operate more effectively with different ones. It is in this sense that the Association may have been considered by some to 'lack policy' while, in fact, the nature of its remit is a very positive one: to fulfil the above-stated purposes, each aspect of which requires the communication and exchange of information rather than the adoption of a single perspective.

It is in this sense also that it may be counter-productive to embrace the view that 'a policy' is even desirable. Rather, our policies have been guided and informed by the Association's aims. This stance not only proceeds from consensus but lends to the decision process that degree of necessary flexibility which is required for responding to the progressively increasing range of issues the Association has to face.

This book thus seeks to further the achievement of the aims of UKRA by raising the question, 'What will be the impact of the National Curriculum on the following issues concerning understanding of the nature and process of reading, the teaching of reading and research into reading?'

1 Development and teaching of reading within the context of literacy and oracy development from pre-school through compulsory schooling and beyond age 16 into the community

2 Recognition of the importance of (a) the findings of completed research and research in progress and (b) investigations to pursue research relating to both theory and classroom-based work

3 Dissemination of research-based information, particularly where it has pertinence across curricular subject areas, home and school, and across phases of schooling

4 Accessibility to general and specialist training in the teaching of literacy in ways that are informed by research and which permit the development of professional skills, including communicative competence with pupils, colleagues and the community: the aim here should be to find a balance between the best of established teaching methods and the findings of the best of research.

The contributors to this book address some of these issues. Our aim is to continue the professional discussion beyond these pages, through conferences, courses, meetings and correspondence as well as publications.

The readability level of the chapters may vary according to readers' purposes, interest and familiarity with the particular context from classroom to research laboratory. Some of the chapters are mainly descriptive, others are prescriptive, some more theoretical, others concrete. Most have a research basis.

A UK Perspective

UKRA members contributing to this book include teachers in primary, secondary and tertiary education, parents, librarians, researchers, psychologists, writers and publishers. It is not solely a response by English and Welsh members. It benefits from the Scottish experience in the wake of the Munn and Dunning reports (SED 1977) which have led to substantial changes in the curriculum in assessment and later in 'Education 10–14 in Scotland' (1986) with its emphasis on continuity between primary and secondary schools.

The recent splendid distillation provided by the Scottish Education Department in its 1989 working paper, 'Curriculum and Assessment in Scotland: A Policy for the '90s: The Balance of the Primary Curriculum', derives from a flow of influential papers all of which place great emphasis on the development of language in context. These include 'Learning and Teaching in Primary 4 and Primary 7' (1980), the COPE Position paper 'Primary Education in the '80s' (1983), 'Some Aspects of Thematic Work in Primary Schools' (1983), 'Learning and Teaching: The Environment and the Primary School Curriculum' (1984).

There have been some significant changes in special education in the UK with the abandonment of the focus on 'handicap' and the adoption in England and Wales of the concept of 'special educational needs' since the Warnock Report of 1978 and related Education Acts which followed. The 1978 HMI Progress Report entitled 'The Education of Pupils with Learning Difficulties in Primary and Secondary Schools in Scotland' and the Joint Consultative Committee on Education in Scotland Report in 1988, 'Ten Years On', illustrate the Scottish approach to the curriculum in emphasising the cross-curricular focus on learning and consequently the need for specialist trained teachers whose role includes cross-curricular consultancy with colleagues as well as co-operative teaching and other responsibilities in the course of their work with pupils with learning difficulties. The value of the consultancy role has not yet been widely recognised throughout the UK.

It is to be hoped that with the introduction of the National Curriculum in England and Wales there will be, increasingly, both appreciation and recognition of the special professional skills which are shared by many special needs and primary school teachers, which are in fact required in all teachers, particularly for continuity across the primary and secondary phases and to deliver the curriculum appropriately to pupils of all abilities and from all linguistic and cultural backgrounds.

We await with interest the sharing of the products of the major initiatives in curriculum development taking place in the Primary Education Development Project run by the Scottish Education Department in conjunction with the colleges of education and the Scottish Development Project in the Expressive Arts by COPE in conjunction with the colleges. Each project is providing resources for teachers. These will include videotapes, resource packs, case studies, policy papers and in-service education materials. As part of the initiatives set up as a result of the 1987 paper on Curriculum and Assessment in the '90s, there are review and development groups in Language, Mathematics, Environmental Studies, Expressive Arts and Religious and Moral Education.

The development of the curriculum within these five areas differs from the approach adopted in the Department of Education and Science policy documents which focus on three 'core' subject areas of English, Mathematics and Science and seven 'other foundation' subjects, History, Geography, Technology (including Design), Music, Art, Physical Education and Religious Education. (A Modern Foreign Language is obligatory only in Key Stages 3 and 4, roughly the secondary school ages 12–16.)

The discussion between UKRA members across the borders within the UK may contribute to the spirit of fostering attitudes which are prerequisite for the kind of balanced and harmonious working towards international literacy at all levels that is one of the aims we share with our parent association, the International Reading Association, and other affiliates including the European Reading Associations and the Australian and Asian Associations. It is hoped the discussions and professional exchange will enrich the development of Primary English in the National Curriculum in England and Wales.

References

Donaldson, M. (1989) 'Sense and Sensibility: Some Thoughts on the Teaching of Literacy.' Centre for Information on Language and Reading, University of Reading.

Scottish Education Department (1977) *The Structure of the Curriculum in the Third and Fourth Years of the Scottish Secondary School* (The Munn Report) and *Assessment for All* (The Dunning Report). HMSO, Edinburgh.

2 Bullock and Kingman: Continuity or Change?

Sarah Tann and Doug Dennis

The Kingman Committee's task relates to a fine history of official documents about English in England, reaching back to the 1921 Newbolt Report, *The Teaching of English* and including the Bullock Report, *Language for Life*, over half a century later (DES, 1975). In 1988 the Committee produced their *Report on the Inquiry into the Teaching of English Language* (the Kingman Report). They did not see their task as revisiting 'the territory so thoroughly traversed by the Bullock Committee' as it would be 'pointless, 12 years later and in changed circumstances' (Kingman, para. 1.10).

If Kingman sees it as 'pointless' to traverse the same ground despite 'changed circumstances', the following questions may be raised. What were the circumstances in each case? What has changed? What is the significance of what has continued, as well as what has changed? Have the circumstances so changed that the philosophy of the Bullock Report is no longer valid? We propose to deal with these questions under the following broad headings:

1 Circumstances and changes
2 Differences between the reports
3 Solutions offered by the reports

Circumstances and Changes

These can be considered in terms of a number of background factors: the concerns evidenced in current reports on educational practices, the educational environments, the research bases upon which the committees could draw, and the nature and provision of training and staff development.

The Evidence from Educational Practice

The Bullock Committee was set up in the aftermath of the 'Black Papers' of 1969 and 1970 which were so strongly critical of the so-called progressive teaching techniques which were supposedly threatening the standards of education in our schools. In addition, the National Foundation for Educational Research report *The Trend in Reading Standards* (Start and Wells, 1972) had further ignited concern, to the extent that the then Secretary of State for Education, Margaret Thatcher, instigated the Bullock enquiry.

The Kingman Committee was also set up following concern over standards and teaching methods as a result of 'observable deficiencies' identified in the HMI reports (such as DES, 1978 and 1979). Some responses to such practices were articulated in such documents as the (1984a) White Paper, 'Better Schools', and also in the report, on *Teaching Quality* (which focused on teacher education), and HMI's initial proposals for the teaching of English in *English from 5 to 16* (DES, 1984b) and its modifications contained in *English from 5 to 16: Responses* (1986).

The Education Environment

The decade prior to the Bullock Report had been characterised as one of considerable curriculum experimentation. This was led by national Schools Council projects as well as local initiatives. Teachers were heavily involved in these initiatives which were very often started at the 'grassroots'.

In stark contrast, the Kingman Committee was set up after some of the most bitter years of teacher industrial action, severe cuts, contraction due to falling rolls, and a series of government-inspired changes intended to touch almost every aspect of the education system, but from which teachers had felt increasingly excluded in terms of negotiating their shape or implementation.

The Research Environment

The 1970s had seen a great deal of interest in alternative techniques for the teaching of reading in the post i.t.a. era, including structured direct-teaching, various approaches based on 'phonics' and a range of so-called language experience approaches. In the 1980s, amidst a proliferation of language programmes, the great debate had moved to the role of 'real books' as opposed to reading schemes.

The 1970s had also seen an increase in interest in the nature of reading in the 'subject/content areas' and the idea of the existence of the 'intermediate skills' (Merritt, 1974) which could be improved by training. In the 1980s this had moved on to more detailed appreciation of the differences between fiction and non-fiction texts and to identifying the text features which posed the greatest difficulty for children.

The 1970s were also caught up in the renewed interest in language structure. Transformational grammars were being used to examine the interrelation of forms and functions of language in new ways. This had extended by the 1980s to examining the oral as well as the written structures of languages, as used by children, adults and different socio-cultural groups (Wilkinson, Stratta and Dudley, 1974). The criterion for evaluating language was changing from 'accuracy' to 'appropriateness'. Furthermore, the unit of linguistic analysis in children's productive language was changing from the word and sentence to the whole text in both fiction and non-fiction genres and in both spoken and written forms (Sinclair and Coulthard, 1975; Stubbs, 1983). Similarly, the interest in children's receptive language (for example, as evident in their reading behaviour, comprehension and response to text) was also shifting from words and sentences to whole texts (Halliday and Hasan, 1976; Chapman, 1987). Attention was increasingly being given to an awareness of historical, geographic and social variations in language, rather than to an exclusive focus on Standard English (Trudgill, 1975; Sutcliffe, 1983; Hawkins, 1984; Freeborn et al., 1986; Crystal, 1988).

Finally, the 1970s witnessed the continuing debate about the role of English – whether it constituted a separate curricular area 'subject content', whether it should be seen as 'process' for individual expression or if and how the balances could be achieved. Different values underpinned the different viewpoints – such as the content emphasis within the 'cultural heritage' approach in the tradition of Leavis (1970) or 'the language as a focus of study' approach (Quirk, 1968), or the process emphasis within the 'language for personal development' (Dixon, 1967; Wilkinson et al., 1980), 'language for life' and 'language as an instrument for learning' (Doughty et al., 1971; Torbe, 1976). The debate also embraced issues such as whether the subject had clear boundaries, or whether it should not create or impose boundaries as they could curtail the individual's experience of language. The expansive, experimental, confident mood had in many places evaporated and been replaced by demands for 'back to basics' – though what those basics were and whether they had ever been abandoned or how they should be developed was still hotly disputed (Knott, 1986).

These are all issues which the Kingman Report recognises. In so doing, the Report also roundly rejects those who argue exclusively for any of the available extreme positions to the exclusion of any other, preferring to combine what it believes to be the strengths from each.

Nature and Provision of Teacher Education and Development

The decade prior to the Bullock Report had been one of great changes. In England it had seen teacher training change from a 2-year to a 3-year course and eventually to a 4-year degree programme of pre-service teacher education. In the UK context, this brought it into line with the Scottish education system where, since 1931, teachers had had 3 years' training or 1 year's post-graduate training (Cruickshank, 1970). There had also been a shift of emphasis from practical professional preparation to additional, more academically rigorous studies in education as a discipline in its own right. This was partly in response to the Ministry of Education pamphlet 'Training Teachers' (1957) which argued for increased rigour and range of studies as part of the intending teacher's 'personal education'. At the same time, English as a subject of study became more literature orientated to distinguish it from the 'professional' language courses which all students followed. By the time of the Kingman Report, the tendency to separate 'theory' from 'practice' had already been criticised and resulted in more integration between the two, in an increasingly classroom-based, reflective model where theory informed practice and practice generated theory.

Further changes in pre-service education were introduced as a result of the publication of the CATE (Council for Accreditation of Teacher Education) criteria (DES, 1985). In particular, these established norms for the proportion of time to be spent on 'second/main subject' and 'professional/education studies' and also the amount of time to be spent on different components of the professional studies.

This period between the Bullock and Kingman reports also witnessed widespread changes affecting in-service education in England. A typical pattern of one-term to one-year in-service courses for seconded teachers, often offered (and funded) by LEAs or in local teaching education 'provider' institutions, has been largely disbanded. It is now being replaced by school-based initiatives funded by monies given to individual schools under the new Local Management by Schools (LMS) formulae. In some areas this appears to have encouraged one-off day conferences for neighbouring schools which allow little depth, little follow-up and little respite for teachers to stand back from their classrooms and reflect.

Differences between the Bullock and Kingman reports

Despite the different circumstances it is interesting to note both the similarities and the differences between the two reports in terms of the parameters and definition of the problems, the foci of the investigations and the solutions recommended.

Parameters of the Bullock and Kingman Reports

Whilst Bullock was set up to review reading standards, and extended this to reviewing a 'language for life', Kingman was set up primarily to investigate HMIs' suggestion (DES, 1984b) that children (and therefore teachers) needed 'to know about language'. This was in response to the widespread objections raised against what some feared might mean a return to traditional sentence-based, Latin-based grammar. Such a return was exactly what Newbolt had warned against (recommendations, 84, 86, 87).

However, the Secretary of State for Education had identified a 'particular gap' in pupils' knowledge of the workings of the English language (DES press release, 16 January 1987). Yet strangely, this particular gap was apparently not identified in any of the HMI reports of 1978 and 1979, nor by the surveys completed by the Assessment Performance Unit (1981–7, set up on the recommendation of Bullock).

Foci of Investigations in the Reports

The main focus of Bullock was on the standards of language in schools and in particular of reading. In common with Bullock and as part of that concern with standards, Kingman focuses on the importance of knowledge about language as a means of improving those standards.

The value of knowledge 'about language' and of the usefulness of 'some technical terms' – or a metalanguage – is not new to Kingman. Both reports suggest that knowledge about language helps the child to master language and use it appropriately and effectively. We need to ask on the basis of what research can such claims be substantiated, and, in order to achieve this, what model of language and what knowledge about language is most suitable. It is this knowledge which is the central focus of the Kingman Report.

The model of language outlined in the Kingman Report is described as a model of 'language in use'. Chapter Two of the Report identifies three aspects of the model of language (its uses, forms and functions) which relate to three functions of adults' language (political, economic and social), four modes of language (reading, writing, talking and listening), and four areas of concern for English teachers (children's intellectual, social, personal and aesthetic development).

Further reading of the Report indicates additional aspects which contribute to the background rationale for the importance of knowledge about language in improving children's use of English. This provides the context in which the model (concerned with the study of language) is presented. However, how the model is related to the rationale is not clear. In fact, a note of reservation to the main body of the report is included on this very issue of the relationship between the model and the purpose of language learning and teaching itself.

Already this is a highly complex and ambitious model to propose, but one which recognises the complexity inherent in the task. 'There can be no such things as THE model. Constant flux is inherent in the nature of language. The word "language" is an abstraction . . . Moreover, because language serves as many purposes as there are needs for communication, any model of language must be, to a greater or lesser extent, specific' (Kingman, 2.39).

Before discussing the model in more detail, it is important to clarify what the Kingman Committee appears to mean by a 'model' and what such a model might do. For example, 'model' can be used to mean

- definitive descriptions of language forms, which might be useful in clarifying meanings of terms – what language is – and thus be important to research investigations/policy implementation;
- an ideal type, a perfect example to inspire or to be imitated – why language should be used in a particular way – which may have prescriptive connotations or evaluative ones;
- a working guide for practical application and adaption – how language is used in a range of situations – which might also include appropriateness or effectiveness.

The Kingman Report spells out what it means by the term 'model':

In this context, 'model' does not, of course, mean an exemplar that is to be copied, but rather a representation that is appropriate to the purpose in hand, in this case 'a model' that will serve as the basis of how teachers are trained to understand how the English language works and also inform professional discussion on all aspects of English teaching. (Kingman, 1.13)

Given this less ambitious use of the term, it is pointless to criticise it for what it is not – the perfect, exemplary model of language. The Kingman Report's representation of language in use is a complex mixture of variables including structure, function and values, as well as the part that language can play in a child's development and in its later adult life. It recognises the pervasive importance of 'language' and does not restrict attention to the narrower concerns of 'English'. It makes central the significance of the place of language across the whole school curriculum, in the child's development and for life. It raises many problems and issues which it certainly does not solve and which must be addressed by all involved with improving the quality of classroom learning.

Such a model, which tries to encompass so many central concerns, is bound to be complex and approximate. In response to such a model it is important to ask whether it is appropriate for the purpose for which it is intended – namely, to help teachers raise standards of children's use of English.

So, what is the model? It is in four parts:

- *The forms of the English language* – sounds, letters, words, sentences and how these relate to meaning
- *Communication and comprehension* – how speakers and writers communicate and how listeners and readers understand them
- *Acquisition and development* – how the child acquires and develops language
- *Historical and geographical variation* – how language changes over time, and how languages which are spread over territories differentiate into dialects or indeed into separate languages (Kingman, 3.1)

In considering the model we need to ascertain whether it is both internally and externally valid. First, how does this model relate to goals the Report sets itself? How appropriate is the model in developing knowledge which will help children to become effective users of language or to help teachers to help children? Secondly, how do the four parts of the model relate to what outside research has already identified about children's uses of language – aspects not referred to in the Report – that is, why and how they use it as well as how it develops (Clark, 1976; Tizard and Hughes, 1984; Wells, 1987; Barnes and Todd, 1977)?

Solutions Offered by the Bullock and Kingman Reports

The Bullock Report lists seventeen principal recommendations, of which two relate to pre- and in-service needs; Kingman lists eighteen, of which nine relate to such matters.

What is significant is the large number of recommendations which, thirteen years later, are again being made: the need for a school policy; trained language consultants in each school; adequate provision; and appropriate monitoring. Both reports also suggest increased attention to national research, development and dissemination in a number of areas.

How and What Children are to be Taught

Both reports outline not only why children need to have knowledge about language but how they should be taught it. Both reject the use of learning by rote from textbook exercises (Bullock, 1.10; Kingman, 1.11). Both reports suggest that knowledge about language should not be 'bolted on' but should inform children's language development in the classroom (Kingman, 4.53). This should enable teachers to give 'purposeful attention' in oral (Bullock, 10.4, 10.9) and written modes (Bullock, 11.24–11.26), and to intervene 'constructively and at an appropriate time' (Kingman, 2.28). Precisely what children will need to be taught is defined in the section about entitlement, attainment and assessment (Kingman, Ch. 5): how they are to be taught will no doubt be the job of the 'expert trainers' when they start their 'cascade' in September 1989.

How Teachers are to be Trained

Both Bullock and Kingman agree that a substantial part of a pre-service course for primary and secondary teachers should be devoted to language and especially the study of language structures itself. Detailed suggestions are made concerning the amount of time to be allocated to language, and to the study of language structure in particular (Kingman, 6.4, 6.5, 6.7, 6.8). In addition, suggestions are made as to the content of such courses and the types of assignments.

However, for all CNAA institutions, there will be difficulty in meeting these demands, for the CATE criteria for both course content and time allocation, as they stand at present, pose severe logistical problems. Further, the changing emphasis will also require considerable time and money for staff development.

As regards in-service education, Kingman suggests the government should give a high priority to language. It also recognises the difficulty under the system of school-based funding that exists in funding secondments for staff to attend courses leading to further qualifications. Kingman therefore suggests that alternative formats for in-service work be adopted – namely, a 'distance learning' model – whereby teachers can participate using techniques pioneered, for example, by the Open University, and a 'cascade' model.

National Bodies for Establishing Attainment Targets, Programmes of Study and to Assist in Moderation and Monitoring

Kingman – in common with Bullock – sees rigorous monitoring as of vital importance. There is also some similarity in the approach to monitoring which both committees recommended – and some important differences.

Both reports suggest a system of monitoring which uses a new set of instruments to assess a wider range of attainments. The Task Group on Assessment and Testing (TGAT) Report (to which Kingman subscribes) includes the idea of standardised assessment tasks which should be introduced as an integral part of teaching and therefore be responsive to the curriculum. Both reports suggest that test materials should be drawn from a bank or pool and be responsive to the changing curriculum.

Differences emerge as to when and how testing should be carried out. These differences reflect the differences in the purpose of testing as conceived in the two reports. Bullock suggests that assessment should take place at 11 and 15 years (rather than 7, 11, 14 and 16), and should be a 'light sampling' to be used to check whether overall standards of the education system were being maintained.

The Kingman Report must be seen in conjunction with the Government's declared aim to establish national testing for every child, so that individual (diagnostic) progress can be monitored as well as inter-school (comparative) ratings be made. Given the tensions that must exist between these two aims (such as the complexity of detail required to be useful in order to fulfil the first aim and the advantages for simplicity in order to be able to handle the enormous burden inherent in the second aim), it is difficult to see how the same system of assessment can serve two such different purposes.

Finally, there are marked differences in the aspects of children's language which are to be assessed. Bullock's emphasis appears to be more on the overall use of the child's language, to give more attention to the process of learning in which language is used (Bullock, 10.24), the strategies for reading (as well as the response to what is read), together with the importance of the child being involved in their own evaluation (8.19). Because these aspects of the child's use of language imply an assessment of that language in use, the methods for assessment, suggested in Bullock, include techniques such as miscue analysis, informal inventories, structured observation and learning diaries (17.18–17.22). Such techniques can be an invaluable source of information to the teacher and the child, for diagnostic purposes. They are not, however, 'systematic' enough to use for comparative purposes such as the Kingman Report implies.

The Kingman Report provides very specific detail on what should be assessed at specific ages (7, 11, 16). Targets are divided into those which indicate what children should be able to do (implicitly 'knowledge how' competences which underly the child's use of language) and those which indicate what they should be able to understand (explicitly 'knowledge about' understandings rather than explanations and definitions . . .) (Kingman, 5.6).

It seems that the child's implicit knowledge and use of language will be formally assessed (presumably by the standardised assessment tasks and tests, to comply with the TGAT proposals, if they are accepted), but the explicit understandings which the child will rationalise and reflect upon will be assessed by the teachers (presumably by ways of observing learning to be outlined later). The more difficult task is left for the teachers who, we are told, do not have sufficient knowledge about language.

Both reports warn against the 'backwash' effect of testing and the possible 'narrowing of experience' (Kingman, 5.14). For these reasons they suggest that testing should be defined as broadly as possible (Kingman, 5.12). Kingman argues that teachers need to be able to identify where pupils need help and therefore 'at 7 it is not too early; deferred it may be too late' (5.13).

However, it is the purposes of testing which still seem to be confused. Remembering the framework offered by Kingman as to the importance of language and the importance of the study of language (three aspects of adult life, four aspects of English teachers' concerns and the demand of four dimensions of language), we are also told that the targets are to meet the 'social purposes of education and the needs for personal development' (entry to higher education, employment, bringing up children) and to meet 'the criteria of the model of language' (Kingman, 5.5).

The Report itself identifies a number of areas in which more information is needed. It is up to the profession to contribute to this analysis and development. Contributions can be made both at the level of pure research by academics and practising classroom teachers, and in terms of applied investigations which will help to implement and disseminate findings throughout the schools – where they belong. There is already relevant on-going research being undertaken in institutions of higher education and also developments within teacher groups sponsored by LEAs and professional organisations such as UKRA. Such efforts need to be intensified in teacher training institutions, education departments and schools, so that those most closely involved in developing classroom practice can play a positive role.

Need change always involve conflict? It certainly involves challenges. We must meet the challenges and do our best to ensure that the changes are demonstrably good for the children and for all those who work for improvements in education, improvements which can be clearly stated, delineated and communicated within a coherent whole philosophy of entitlement to education.

References

Adams, A. and Jones, E. (1989) *English Teaching Programme and Policy.* Open University Press, Milton Keynes.

Assessment Performance Unit (1988) *Language Performance in Schools: A Review of APU Language Monitoring, 1979–83.* HMSO, London.

Barnes, D. and Todd, F. (1977) *Communication and Learning in Small Groups.* Routledge Kegan Paul, London.

Chapman, J. (1987) *Reading for 5 to 11 Years.* Open University Press, Milton Keynes.

Clark, M. (1976) *Young Fluent Readers.* Heinemann, London.

Cox, C. B. and Dyson, A. E. (1969) *Black Paper One: Fight for Education.* Critical Quarterly Society, London.

Cox, C. B. and Dyson, A. E. (1970) *Black Paper Two: The Crisis in Education.* Critical Quarterly Society, London.

Cruikshank, M. (1970) *A History of the Training of Teachers in Scotland.* University of London Press, London.

Crystal, D. (1988) *The English Language.* Penguin, London.

Department of Education and Science (1975) *Language for Life* (The Bullock Report). HMSO, London.

Department of Education and Science (1978) *Primary Education in England.* HMSO, London.

Department of Education and Science (1979) *Aspects of Secondary Education.* HMSO, London.

Department of Education and Science (1982) *Education 5–9: An Illustrative Survey of 80 First Schools in England.* HMSO, London.

Department of Education and Science (1983a) *Middle Schools: An Illustrative Survey*. HMSO, London.
Department of Education and Science (1983b) *Teaching Quality*. HMSO, London.
Department of Education and Science (1984a) *Better Schools*. HMSO, London.
Department of Education and Science (1984b) *English from 5 to 16: Curriculum Matters 1*. HMSO, London.
Department of Education and Science (1985) *CATE Note 1*. HMSO, London.
Department of Education and Science (1986) *English from 5 to 16: Responses*. HMSO, London.
Department of Education and Science (1988a) *Report of the Committee of Inquiry into the Teaching of the English Language* (The Kingman Report). HMSO, London.
Department of Education and Science (1988b) *English for Ages 5 to 11* (The first Cox Report). HMSO, London.
Department of Education and Science (1989) *English for Ages 5 to 16* (The second Cox Report). HMSO, London.
Department of Education and Science (undated) *Task Group on Assessment and Testing: A Report*. DES/WO, London.
Dixon, J. (1967) *Growth through English*. Oxford University Press, Oxford.
Doughty, P., Pearce, J. and Thornton, G. (1971) *Language in the Schools*. Edward Arnold, London.
Freeborn, D. et al. (1986) *Varieties of English*. Macmillan, Basingstoke.
Halliday, M. A. K. and Hasan, R. (1976) *Cohesion in English*. Longman, London.
Hawkins, E. (1984) *Awareness of Language*. Cambridge University Press, Cambridge.
Jones, M. and West, A. (eds) (1988) *Learning me your Language*. Mary Glasgow, London.
Knott, R. (1985) *The English Department in a Changing World*. Open University Press, Milton Keynes.
Leavis, F. R. (1970) *English Literature in our Time and the University*. Chatto and Windus, London.
Merritt, J. (1974) *A Grammar of Contemporary English*. Longman, London.
Quirk, R. (1972) 'The Intermediate Skills' in Morris, J. M. *The First R*. UKRA/Ward Lock Educational, London.

Sinclair, J. and Coulthard, B. (1975) *Towards an Analysis of Discourse*. Oxford University Press, Oxford.

Start, K. B. and Wells, B. (1972) *The Trend of Reading Standards*. NFER, Slough.

Stubbs, M. (1983) *Discourse Analysis*. Basil Blackwell, Oxford.

Sutcliffe, D. (1982) *British Black English*. Basil Blackwell, Oxford.

Thornton, G. (1986) *APU Language Testing, 1979–83: An Independent Appraisal of Findings*. DES, London.

Tizard, B. and Hughes, M. (1984) *Young Children Learning*. Fontana, London.

Torbe, M. (1976) *Language across the Curriculum*. Ward Locke for NAPE, London.

Trudgill, P. (1975) *Accent, Dialect and the School*. Edward Arnold, London.

Wells, G. (1987) *The Meaning Makers*. Hodder and Stoughton, Sevenoaks.

Wilkinson, A. (1975) *Language and Education*. Oxford University Press, Oxford.

Wilkinson, A., Stratta, L. and Dudley, P. (1974) *The Quality of Listening*. Macmillan, Basingstoke.

Wilkinson, A., Barnsley, G., Hanna, P. and Swan, M. (1980) *Assessing Language Development*. Oxford University Press, Oxford.

3 English in the National Curriculum: Getting the Time Right

Ronald Arnold

English in the National Curriculum is taking shape rather like one of those pictures which you create by joining the dots. All the lines are now in place, and we can see what the picture is saying, but we cannot yet ink it in. Still, we have seen enough of the consultation process so far to know that, though there may be some minor changes, *English for ages 5 to 16* will remain largely intact. It retains the spirit, the central beliefs, and most of the detail of its predecessor, *English for ages 5 to 11*. We all knew that the Secretary of State would insist on 'greater emphasis on pupils' mastery of the grammatical structure of the English language', but even that insistence was tempered by right thinking. What happened between the Draft Orders and the Final Orders is worth pausing on for a moment if only because it tells us something important about the prevailing spirit of things. In the Draft Orders for Key Stage 1 we are told that 'teachers should . . . teach terms like punctuation, letter, capital letter, full stop, question mark' and that pupils 'should be taught grammatical terms like sentence, verb, tense, noun, pronoun'. By the time the Final Orders emerge, only weeks later, these have become: 'Teachers should *introduce pupils* to terms such as punctuation, letter, capital letter, full stop, question mark' and 'they [the pupils] should be taught, *in the context of discussion about their own writing*, grammatical terms such as sentence, verb, tense, noun, pronoun' (my italics). More of the practical implications of this later, but for the present let us take heart that a good tune can get through even to the unmusical.

We need to seek out, magnify, and proclaim all the many good things in English in the National Curriculum, for there is no opting out of it. Indeed, it can be summed up in a Russian proverb and in a remark of Winston Churchill's; respectively: 'If the river freezes you must learn to skate', and 'It is not enough to do what we like. We must like what we do.' And there is plenty to like, for *English for ages 5 to 16* presents an excellent rationale for the teaching of English, and it supports this with equally excellent programmes of study. It represents in rich detail the best developments in the subject over the years, and it reflects the best advice in the field. It quickly goes to the heart of good practice by saying that this exists where pupils:

- use language to make, receive, and communicate meaning, in purposeful contexts;
- employ a variety of spoken and written forms with a clear awareness of audience;
- work on tasks which they have chosen and which they direct for themselves;
- work with teachers who are themselves actively involved in producing language – as talkers, listeners, readers and writers;
- read literature for enjoyment, responding to it critically and using their reading for learning.

Unfortunately, more was required of the Report than that. It had to propose attainment targets which fitted into the framework devised by the Task Group on Assessment and Testing (TGAT). The two aspects of *English for ages 5 to 16* sit together uneasily, and the working group has not managed to weld them into a convincing whole. The discomfort sets in when the profile components are translated into attainment targets and the targets are anatomised into 'strands', with the obligation to arrive at the right 'level' when assessing how well they have been met. There is no doubt at all that the notion of assigning pupils to levels, and doing it accurately and fairly, is what is worrying teachers most of all. And well it might, if we are to take seriously the original document *The National Curriculum 5 to 16*, of July 1987: 'Parents will be able to judge their children's progress against agreed national targets for attainment and will also be able to judge the effectiveness of their school', and other such statements. There would be some consolation if the levels were all that they might be; but they are not. The differences between them sometimes seem arbitrary, as they are bound to when those charged with framing them are faced with such problems of definition and gradation.

The real matter for concern, though, is that targets concentrate the eye wonderfully, to the exclusion of peripheral vision. Given the pressure that teachers are feeling, it would not be surprising if they focused intensely on the targets, and on the levels within them, at the expense of the programmes of study and of those excellent chapters which underpin those programmes. Indeed, there is every encouragement to do this when *English for ages 5 to 16* makes a point of printing the targets and the programmes of study ahead of all the other chapters, in contrasting colour at that, and then of printing the targets ahead of the programmes. The worst thing that could happen to English in the National Curriculum is that the spirit of its programmes of study becomes obliterated by a narrow interpretation of its attainment targets. For let us make no mistake about it, the National Curriculum will flourish or founder, be fulfilled or frustrated, on the strength of the teacher's interpretation of it within each classroom.

I have no doubt that it will flourish and be fulfilled, because there are many thousands of people determined to see it serve the best interests of children. But it will need a sharing of enthusiasm and ideas, and the steady building of confidence. There are still many children whose view of language is one of hurdles to be braved, and whose weekly experience is one of prescriptive attitudes, emphasis on the correction of faults, and punitive marking. If 'knowledge about language' becomes another of their burdens, without abatement of any of the others, then they will have little to thank the National Curriculum for.

Knowledge about language is taken very seriously in *English for ages 5 to 16*, to the extent that all the statements of attainment that refer to it, in all the profile components, are extracted, collected together, and put on show. It is worth reminding ourselves of a key sentence in the Kingman Report, to which this list owes much. 'If a move from spontaneous practice to considered reflection is sensitively handled by the teacher, it becomes quite natural to talk about language in classrooms.' The teacher is asked to 'intervene constructively', which is very close to Bullock's call for 'planned intervention'. Indeed, the antecedents of this explicit attention to language are all there in the Bullock Report, which is worth quoting to show the lineage: 'Curiosity about language is widespread among children . . . The teacher encourages this curiosity and seizes the opportunity of pursuing some general questions about language as it arises from usage, collecting and organising further examples for the purposes of answering the question.'

The endorsement of knowledge about language within the National Curriculum must not be allowed to encourage the use of textbook exercises. There is a vast amount of evidence to show that such methods are unproductive. Rice made the point as early as 1903, and the research evidence has since accumulated to reinforce it, that the working of exercises as a discrete activity is peculiarly valueless. The Bullock Report agreed the case in these words: the child's development of writing ability

can be expressed in terms of increasing differentiation. He or she learns to carry his use of English into a much broader range of situation, to differing kinds of audience. The purposes to which he puts language grow more complex, so that he moves from a narrative level of organising experience to one where he is capable of sustained generalisation. Considered in these terms the handling of language is a complex ability, and one that will not be developed simply by working through a series of textbook exercises.

Nor will a knowledge about language be developed in that way. What we want to see is language brought to the fore of classroom discussion, with children enthused about it, learning more about it, and freely able to talk about it. The active discussion of language at work can start early in the child's school life and should be an established way of working throughout the primary years. Children should learn to work collectively on language, discussing the varying of effects in their own work with the same confidence with which they become used to discussing other writing. They can be shown, for example, that in good writing there is a curious kind of alchemy at work which endows a word with overtones according to the company it keeps. Words take on connotations from the way they are placed within contexts, and they radiate influences upon other words. When pupils study the workings of language in such ways their command of the metalanguage grows naturally. The teacher's assessment will aim to produce a body of knowledge about each child's performance and understanding from which decisions can be made on where he or she needs to be taken next. It will be for the teacher to decide whether a particular child or group of children is at the right point for, say, some attention to be given to particular lexical or syntactical features. These should not then be taught *in vacuo* but should emerge at the teacher's prompting during the natural and accustomed process of discussing language at work. Thus, the teacher's role would be to build up a repertoire of understandings about language at the same time as stimulating kinds of writing which will create a need for their use.

In this regard, primary school teachers are presented with unique opportunities, arising from the fact that they are still responsible for the work of the class across the whole, or at any rate the greater part, of the curriculum. Five minutes with the programmes of study reveal how copious these opportunities are, for the primary curriculum provides an unlimited variety of contexts in which reading, writing and talk can be developed. There should be no need for imposed writing tasks, for example, except for special reasons at special times. When the work of a primary classroom is in full surge, the stimulus to write is everywhere, and the wider the range of classroom experience the greater the variety of writing it gives rise to.

The same is true of reading. The best way to improve reading standards is to fill the school with books and to place no embargoes on when, in what numbers, and in what variety they may be read. There will be plenty of good fiction, but there will also be plenty of non-fiction titles which answer to as wide a range of the children's interests as possible. The greater the quantity and the more extensive the range, the more likely it is that the interest generated anywhere in the curriculum can be fulfilled and followed up. And it should be followed up in talk. The entire curriculum is material for talking and listening. All those oral language skills that the National Curriculum promotes can be developed in just about every area of learning. And conversely, in no area can learning be really effective unless those skills are engaged.

English in the National Curriculum is there for the seizing. Language has great fascination, and it can be a source of enjoyment, fulfilment, and self-possession. It can also be a source of disappointment, frustration, and a poor self-image. We know what we can make of it, and we know what it must be.

4 Should English Teachers Teach Grammar?

Colin Harrison

Why Do We Teach Grammar?

There is an enormous weight of received opinion, public pressure, and tradition which presses down upon teachers of language arts, and which produces apparently cogent and undoubtedly forceful arguments in favour of teaching grammar as a central focus of the language arts curriculum.

The main explanation for why language arts teachers teach grammar rests on the opinion that many people hold that a study of grammar helps someone to speak and to write better English. This in turn, people feel, increases their employment prospects and life chances.

These opinions are powerfully expressed by employers, administrators, broadcasters, newspaper editors and authors, most of whom were taught grammar themselves, and who believe that there is a causal relationship between their fluency in English and their having been taught grammar. Parents too, whether or not they are skilled and confident language users, tend to hold equally strongly to the view that the learning of grammar is integral to becoming an expert speaker or writer.

Later in this paper I shall argue that in many respects these beliefs, while understandable, are ill-founded. They are not, however, the only imperatives which act to keep grammar a primary focus of the language arts curriculum. Within schools, other teachers will argue that if language arts teachers aren't teaching grammar, they are shirking a duty, and acting in a professionally irresponsible manner. Modern languages teachers are often particu-

This is a revised version of an article which first appeared in the *Virginia English Bulletin*.

larly scathing towards English teachers who fail to teach grammar, or who fail to teach it effectually. They bemoan the fact that they have to teach two grammars, that of English and that of the language for which they are responsible.

Finally, there is the weight of tradition. For decades, grammar has been a key element in language arts teaching. Textbooks and workbooks which focus on grammar are in nearly every school, and offer work at nearly every grade level. Tradition thus becomes institutionalised as part of a massive industry. At the same time, teachers who may doubt the efficacy of grammar books have become accustomed to using them. The tradition is also a comfort, offering teachers a subtle but possibly insidious assurance: trust me, it whispers, for whether it is effective or not, it will keep children's activity on task. The study of grammar here serves reciprocal sets of interests – it keeps textbook sales up, and students' heads down. An admirable symbiosis.

Why We Should Not Teach Grammar

1 It Doesn't Work

The primary reason for not teaching grammar is the obverse of the primary reason most people believe it should be taught. For, contrary to what received opinion might suggest, it is by no means certain that being taught grammar improves a person's spoken or written language. Carefully controlled large-scale experimental studies in English-speaking countries from the USA to New Zealand have failed to show any greater improvement in language use when 'grammar' versus 'no grammar' classes have been compared.

How is it that such research results can come to be ignored? One powerful reason is perhaps the momentum (or is it inertia?) generated by the textbook industry, but I am not wishing to argue that a conspiracy is acting to suppress the implications of the research findings. What is more probably the case is that decision makers in education have accepted the causal fallacy I referred to earlier: namely they feel that in their own experience it has been valuable to be aware of grammatical rules, and that therefore such knowledge would be, and should be available to all students.

What this view fails to take account of is the problem that grammar is a highly abstract (and in certain respects arbitrary) system for representing the structural relationships in a language. To have an understanding of how this system works is certainly an asset, just as having an understanding of linear algebra can be valuable to a person who needs to solve everyday problems of arithmetic, but this does not imply that it can be taught successfully to everyone. From the point of view of developmental psychology, formal grammar study requires formal reasoning, in the Piagetian sense, just as surely as a study of logic requires formal reasoning. From this perspective, it is small wonder that many students learn little from it, and fail to apply what they do learn. What I wish to argue is that for most children in school, at least before they reach year eleven, a study of grammar is irrelevant and potentially counterproductive. They can't understand it, even if they acquire some automated procedures which make it look as if they do. Worse than that, it has two very damaging effects: it turns children off English, and it teaches them to feel negatively about their own culture and language.

2   *It Turns Children off English*

One really sad aspect of how we teach grammar is that it transforms the view many students have of the business of writing.

Children who love reading, and delight in their new-found ability to write their own stories, can be heard saying, 'I hate English!' The first time I heard this from my own child, I couldn't believe my ears. Chrissie was nine years old; he loved stories, he loved drama, but most of all he loved to write. He would write sagas ten pages long, mostly highly derivative spy/detective stories, full of A-team explosions and Magnum car chases.

It turned out, of course, that by 'English' he meant the statutory three sessions per week spent doing exercises from a book of grammar and comprehension exercises. I would seriously question whether he learned anything from doing those exercises, apart from an aversion to the concept of 'English'. As I left England in September 1986, for a three-month visit to the USA, Chris was about to begin comprehensive school. He was full of enthusiasm. 'I hope there'll be lots of creative writing,' he said. I said I hoped so, too, but inside I felt a stab of certainty that the exercises would be continued, probably with an increased dosage.

3 It Fosters Cultural Elitism

Although they have some generative properties, most formal grammars are descriptive rather than prescriptive; they describe how our language functions, and do not claim to prescribe how it should function. But grammar, as it is taught in our schools, is not merely descriptive, it is prescriptive. It is prescriptive in ways that are often deeply damaging to the very students it is supposed to help.

What children learn from their teachers is that their grammar is bad. They learn that how they speak and write is not just different from how the teacher speaks and writes, it is 'wrong'. From the point of view of contemporary linguistics, this is an astounding state of affairs. By the time they have reached the age of five, practically all children have acquired a perfect command of the grammar of their language. No matter how highly motivated you are, and how long you work at it, the chances are that you will never become as fluent in a second language as just about all students are in the language with which they enter school. They will speak it with an accent, and will have dialect variations, but these are inevitable: everyone speaks with an accent, and with dialect variations. We now recognise that no one speaks Standard English (or speaks it with 'Received Pronunciation', for that matter); these notions are constructs which are useful in discussion about language, but they cannot be applied to the language performance of native speakers of the language, even if those speakers happen to come from Inverness!

The fact that nearly every child begins school fluent and grammatically perfect in their native language is an achievement unparalleled by any subsequent successes attributable to the education system. An untrained task force of parents, grandparents, siblings, baby-minders and friends achieves greater success than we as teachers will achieve in teaching reading or in teaching a second language. Granted, the brain's learning capacity for language acquisition is at its best in those early years, but my point is that we tend to dismiss those considerable gains, or even act as if we regard them as unfortunate. In the sixties and seventies there was a good deal of discussion about the concept of linguistic diversity, and many teachers made, and now continue to make, great efforts to be creative in their teaching, in order to celebrate the richness of that diversity. What I would suggest is that grammar teaching which begins and ends with the view that to say 'ain't' is wrong, that to use a double negative is wrong, and that to write using the verb 'got' is wrong, may be seriously counterproductive. No wonder students go straight out to the playground and continue to use the language with which they are familiar; such language has equal or better communicative effectiveness, and it does not introduce a social distance between speakers, which is what would happen if a child actually *did* stop saying 'ain't'. (Think, for example, of what happened when you got to college: didn't you drop a regional accent – and then find yourself busily reconstructing it when you came home on vacation, so that people wouldn't think you were putting on airs?)

What I would argue is that instead of teaching the social conventions of our language in this divisive way as part of what we incorrectly call teaching 'grammar', we should have language study as a central focus for our teaching, but approach it in ways very different from those which are rooted in a type of cultural elitism.

Why We Should Study Language

1   Language, Knowledge and Power

English teachers are very familiar with Bacon's maxim that knowledge is power. Those in favour of the teaching of grammar will strongly assert that knowledge of the language gives the user greater power to control it. I fully accept this sentiment, though I cannot accept that teaching grammar will offer many students access to this power. Indeed, to focus solely on the teaching of grammar might be to seriously limit the extent to which many students could gain power over their language.

What I would wish to argue is that systematic study of language, rather than the study of formal grammar, is what can offer all students better opportunities to understand how language is used by them and on them. This in turn can give them more power to use language effectively, and to see it as a tool over which they have control in their own lives, rather than an abstract game whose rules they do not fully comprehend. To this extent, the teaching of language is in a broad sense a political activity. Teaching formal grammar is in most respects uncontentious: grammarians may quibble about the adequacy of descriptive systems, but politicians and administrators will not feel that their territory is threatened. By contrast, consider what happens if the object of language study becomes the relationship between language and the world: the only rationale for doing this is to empower students to change their world.

The question now becomes not 'Why teach grammar?' but 'Why teach children to become more skilled language users?', and the answer is not 'In order to produce more English graduates in university', but 'In order to produce adults who can use their understanding of language to do such things as to question explanations that are inadequate, to spot bias, to run a meeting confidently, to criticise advertisements thoughtfully, and to handle relationships skillfully'.

2 Power over what?

Much study of formal grammar makes little use of the knowledge the student already possesses. I have already suggested that this knowledge is considerable, even in the case of a young child entering formal schooling, and I would submit that it should be the starting point for the systematic study of language. If the student's own language experience is the starting point, then we circumvent the problems which arise from analysing the properties of a purely formal system. The depth of analysis which is called for might be great, but if the starting point is in the concrete and the known, it will not be inaccessible. Thus, instead of trying to eradicate usages such as double negatives, on the spurious logic that two negatives make a positive (does this mean that the French academicians are wrong to use both *ne* and *pas*?), we might consider investigating the ways in which native language users spontaneously demonstrate a sophisticated knowledge of the language system, for example when they shift linguistic register. This would certainly involve a systematic attention to alternative forms of utterance, but it builds upon the fact that children are already sensitive to the need to adapt their language in this way, whether they have realised it or not.

A 'register' is a context-bound subset of a language, and even if we choose not to use this term, children will readily accept that people vary their expression according to the situation. They know that ordinarily no one would say, 'I live in a desirable residence in Reston.' That phrase belongs to the linguistic register of the real estate agent. They will be equally aware of who might use the word 'pad' but who could suggest when the word 'domicile' might be used?

Children who are hardly able to write will be capable of improvising in drama the differences in small talk which occur when first a friend and then the local vicar arrives. Children's sense of audience is acute, and can be the focus of valuable language study. When they sit back to back and improvise a telephone conversation, then rerun the conversation face to face, a great deal of knowledge of linguistic conventions is displayed, and a good teacher will have little difficulty getting the other students to externalise and comment on what is revealed.

Equally, instead of engaging in the hopeless task of attempting to suppress dialect variations, a teacher can simultaneously celebrate these and give students the opportunity to make choices between alternative forms of expression. In England, which still has many fundamentally snobbish attitudes towards regional accents, there have nevertheless been some significant shifts of opinion and action in this field. The BBC now employs newsreaders and announcers with regional accents, and many parts of the country have produced books which are written in, and make a conscious attempt to preserve, regional dialects. These, and some of the many LP records which have been made, offer a basis for constructing language arts activities which examine and lay bare dialect variations, but which do not castigate them as erroneous, irrelevant or unacceptable.

In the novels and short stories of D. H. Lawrence, the dialect of the Nottinghamshire–Derbyshire border is portrayed with great skill, and the dialect of the miners and factory workers is seen to have great vitality and directness. In 1976, within a few miles of where Lawrence was born, a book called *Ey Up Mi Duck!* was published. This celebrates, through cartoons, dialect verse and quizzes, the regional language variations of this part of England. The book was reprinted three times within a year, and the reason is that it was bought, not only by local residents, but by language arts teachers, who made good use of it in their classes. Consider what valuable language study could come out of the following:

1   A list of eighteenth century spelling errors in parish and accounting records including:

chimdey
ingin
markit
owd (old)
shot (shirt)
watter (water)

2   A quiz on local dialect expressions, such as:

ISITIZEN?   (a question of ownership)
TINTAAHN!   (a statement concerning ownership)
ARKATTIT!   (it is raining heavily)
AIRTHIKAYPIN?   (friendly greeting)
AWICKATHOZDEE   (a future appointment)

3   A dialect poem, from which this is an extract:

Wey'd gerrup Sundee mornin
An gerron aht te plee.
It wer stow pot fer yer breakfast
An bread an lard fer tea.
If yer owd man shaated yuh
Yuh doesn't stay on aht–
Yuh knew yo'd ay te dab on in
Or else yo'd gerra claat.

What is enjoyable about undertaking this type of language study is that while it certainly encourages discussion about the appropriateness of local dialect in certain contexts, it also values the language knowledge which the children possess; it recognises their expertise, and puts the teacher in the role of neutral chair of a discussion in which the students are the true experts, since they, and not the instructor, are the native users of that dialect, and are able to speak with authority about its usage and connotations.

What Language Should We Study?

I have suggested that language study should value and utilise the skills and internalised knowledge of students. But this is a starting point, not a curriculum. In this final section I wish to describe in a little more detail the type of activity which I have in mind under the broad heading of systematic language study.

Semiotics, Pragmatics, and Sociolinguistics

The function of language is to communicate. It is a sign system, and how those signs function is central to our understanding of how language works. It is for this reason that I would see semiotics as a perfectly valid part of the language arts curriculum. Traffic signs, advertisements, body language, concrete poetry and graffiti are all instances of topics which could furnish many sessions of study round the issues of how signs transmit messages and ideologies. Try these ideas with your class, but not before you've added some of your own.

- Invent a new body language, including your own signals for 'yes', 'no', greeting – and kissing!
- Invent a set of signals for school; for example, 'Yield for juniors!', or 'Danger! Darren Smith plays "Two Minutes in the Cupboard"!'
- Invent a secret code, and send messages in it.
- Make a survey of the colours of the cars of a group of people you know; what can you learn from this?
- Choose five nations and draw a picture of their national flags: try to find out whether the colours and design of the flags have a special meaning.
- Make a survey of clothing which people wear which has a word or special logo as part of its design. How many different ones can you identify? Why are these words and pictures outside, and not on a label inside?

The term 'pragmatics' refers to a study of those aspects of an utterance which are not part of its surface structure, but which nevertheless affect its meaning, such as intonation, or a context which indicates an ironic inversion of the surface message. Again, children are well aware of these possibilities. As John Holt observed in *How Children Fail* (Penguin, 1969), teachers say 'yes' when they mean 'no', and the student recognises this from the rising and falling tone which really means, 'You're wrong, but keep trying . . .'

One way of getting into some of the educationally valuable possibilities connected with this area, and also touching some good ideas for creative writing, is to work on the topic of hearing, overhearing and deafness. A number of these activities would also invite speculation about the social function of language. Do you consider the following to be worthwhile as ways into language study?

- Try communicating only with sign language for fifteen minutes. Work with a friend, and try to tell a story, tell a joke, and report a sports event. What things were easy/difficult/ impossible to communicate?
- Imagine you lived at the bottom of the sea. What would the world sound like?
- Start a rumour. Did it work?
- In Pumpkin County, communication is difficult, because the word 'pumpkin' is the only one anyone is permitted to use (so everyone is called Pumpkin Pumpkin, and the expression for 'Good morning!' is 'Pumpkin pumpkin!'). Working with a friend prepare a three-minute play in which you either (a) get arrested by a pumpkin for riding your pumpkin on the pumpkin, or (b) have an argument with your pumpkins about whether or not you should be allowed to pumpkin on Saturday night. Remember, the only word you can use in the script is 'pumpkin'. Good luck!

Analysis at the Word and Phrase Level

I would not wish to assert, in questioning the value of teaching formal grammar, that there is no place in the language arts classroom for close attention to how language functions at the word, phrase and sentence level. What I would suggest is that it can be approached much more purposefully, interestingly and collaboratively than is normally done. One approach I use in teaching nine- to twelve-year-olds is through a computer program called Storyboard. This is a type of total cloze or total deletion exercise, and I do it with large groups, up to twenty or more in size. To begin with, what the students see on the VDU is a series of dashes, each of which stands for just one missing letter, like this:

'------, ------!' -------- --. -----.
'---- -----! --- ---- ---- -- ---- -- - ----- -------.
---- -------- --- ---- -- ----- ---- --- ----- ----, ---
- ----- ---- --- ---- --- ------!'

Usually, the text on the screen is about eighteen lines long, which gives rather more punctuation and word-length clues to the possible structure of the message than you have in the sample passage above. What the students have to do is to think of and enter words which they think are in the passage, until the whole story is reconstructed. Someone inputs complete words, one at a time, and each time the computer recognises a word which is in the passage, it updates the screen, and inserts every occurrence of that word. Most English teachers do not like the look of this game at first. They see it as yet another gap-filling activity, based on a rather arbitrary guessing game, and their agnosticism is perfectly justifiable.

In fact, I would submit that there is much more depth to the activity than appears at first sight. The students are told that they are only permitted one hundred guesses in total, and this encourages them to be judicious in their choices. After a few called out suggestions, which locate the most frequently occurring words, such as *a*, *the*, and *and*, I ask the students to form into groups of two or three, and to make a list of their next ten suggestions. I also tell them that I shall ask them to indicate the exact place where they think their word is going to occur. As the screen begins to fill up I ask them to give arguments to support their choices, especially where students disagree about likely contenders for the same spot.

When children play Storyboard (and I have piloted it with children from eight to fifty-eight!), they have to find some basis for constructing cogent arguments which relate to precise grammatical, tonal and stylistic judgments. This they do, yet interestingly they can do so without using the formal terminology of grammar. Children will thoughtfully discuss tenses, number, pronominal reference, adverbial modifiers and synonyms without ever using the technical terms, and without being in the least inhibited by the fact that they do not know them. I even have a vivid recollection of a ten-year-old girl grabbing the arm of a boy a foot shorter than her, who had typed in the word DOCTER and was about to hit the 'Enter' key, and yelling in his ear, 'GET A DICTIONARY!'

Language Study and Literature

One of the unfortunate aspects of the way we teach English is that too often the study of language is divorced from the study of literature. Indeed, we seem to go to great lengths to ensure that the ecological validity of language and reading courses is dismally low. We set grammar exercises on sentences which no human ever spoke, and we give comprehension exercises on texts which no author ever published to be read for their own sake. There are good reasons for this: the sentences we speak break most of the rules of grammar, at least the sort of prescriptive 'grammar' expounded in the English workbook; and it costs a good deal of money to use an extract from a real book in a comprehension exercise, even supposing the author would permit its use.

Yet consider for a moment how much fascinating language work can come naturally from a study of literature. Many children love the stories of the American writers Judy Blume and Betsy Byars. We made a glossary of Americanisms for those who might get stumped by *calling the role* [*sic*], *gotten, cookies, loafers, sixth grade,* and *deli*.

Another possibility is to ask children to write a continuation chapter for a book they enjoyed, or to write a chapter which gives an account in detail of an event which the author only reported briefly. To do this well requires great attention to the prose style of the author, and it invites a much more integrated consideration of how the author writes than a grammar exercise ever could. Equally, I would argue that such activities as writing journals on behalf of the characters in a book, or preparing improvised scenes are language study activities just as surely as they are reading and literacy activities.

Improving Technical Accuracy

Finally, I want to address the important issue of how we help students to learn from what they write, and how we as instructors should respond to the fact that all young writers at times write awkwardly, and punctuate and spell incorrectly. Some schools will teach English using course books with the familiar traditional exercises. Some other schools do not, and yet they produce outstandingly good writers who have never over the twelve years of formal schooling seen a grammar exercise. What do these schools do instead to develop technical accuracy?

1   They believe that children learn to write by writing, so there is a great deal of emphasis on drafting, discussion, collaboration and seeking real audiences for the students' writing.
2   They believe that children learn to write by reading real books,

so in addition to fostering reading through classroom libraries and individual book reports, they will read books aloud in class right up to the end of secondary schooling (even at the expense of doing no other work in class for two weeks or more), and planning and negotiating assignments on the book with the students. They will invite in local authors, taking advantage of an Arts Council's 'Authors in School' funding programme.

3   They believe that generally speaking it is damaging and counterproductive to 'correct' the errors in a piece of creative writing. Before a piece of writing is set, a teacher will make clear whether it is to be corrected and graded for technical accuracy. If it is not, no numerical or alphabetic grade will be given; instead the teacher will respond to the piece as we would if a friend had written a story and asked to comment on it.

4   If a later draft is to be shared with a wider audience, on display or in a newspaper or magazine, the teacher might put the students in a conference with others who would make suggestions concerning accuracy and expression. The teacher would probably, but not necessarily, be the final person to offer comment on possible changes.

5   If a teacher notices a general weakness on some aspect of technical accuracy, he or she might have a twenty-minute blitz on it during class time.

What I wish to emphasise is that there is nothing sentimental or sloppy about the procedure outlined above. The teachers work just as hard as they would if they were marking grammar exercises and correcting punctuation errors. The reason these teachers do not do these things is not because they have a precious view of children, but rather because they believe that setting grammar exercises and wielding a red biro do nothing to improve anyone's writing. They feel that children regard grammar exercises as a chore totally unconnected with the business of real writing, and that they do not learn anything from the many hours teachers devote to the careful correcting of errors in their prose. They glance at the red ink and think, 'I *know* that my "expression was awkward", and that my "punctuation was careless". That's because I'm bad at English.' And they turn to their next task. I would go so far as to say that correcting students' writing, unless it is for some purpose such as preparing it for another audience, is a monumental waste of the English teacher's professional talent.

In the departments whose procedure I was outlining above, this is sometimes written directly as departmental policy, and the newer members of the department are encouraged to try to not feel guilty about only marking for technical accuracy once every few weeks, and to spend the time thus liberated in extending their reading of children's fiction.

Do the practices I am advocating seem revolutionary and/or impossibly idealistic? Let me assure you that they have been operating in many schools for a number of years, and with excellent results, and they are wholly compatible with both Kingman's and Cox's recommendations. I have great respect for the sincerity and professional concern of teachers who believe that it is important to teach grammar, but I do not share their belief, for the reasons I have tried to outline above.

Part II
The Kingman Channel

5 Keeping up with Kingman: What the Newspapers Said

Roger Beard

At one point in the Kingman Report there is an acknowledgement that comparison of the way in which the same event is covered in different newspapers can make pupils realise that 'language can obscure truth as well as reveal it'. It may be a little premature to argue too strongly about the way the national press obscured or revealed 'the truth' of the Report, but it can be instructive and revealing for parents, teachers and other adult commentators to consider how effectively each national newspaper brought this particular item to its sections of the public, if at all . . .

The four million people who bought the *Sun* on Saturday 30 April 1988 did not have the opportunity to hear anything about the *Report of the Committee of Enquiry into the Teaching of English Language*. Nor did the three million who bought the *Daily Mirror* or the one and a quarter million who bought the *Star*.

Of course, Kingman was never going to be featured in main front page headlines but reports of it did make the front pages of the *Independent* and the *Daily Telegraph* and there was a very brief mention on the front page of the *Financial Times* too.

A read of these front-page references indicated not only which papers had dealt with the Report most thoroughly but also provided some memorable touches of the virtuosity of written language – and the challenges to those who try to describe its power and utility: the *Independent* announced, 'Report spells out an English compromise' while the *Daily Telegraph* told us, 'Kingman rules out lessons in grammar'.

For those who delight in the illustrative power of headline puns, there were plenty more to come inside the 'quality' dailies. With *The Times* in sombre mood ('Back to Grammar') and the *Guardian* remarkably pun-free ('English: the uses and the abuses'), it was left to the *Financial Times* to exploit the potential of 'Speaking the

Kingman's English' while the *Independent* carried on with 'Raising English from the dead'. But perhaps it was the *Daily Telegraph* who went ahead on points with 'Speaking up for Kingman and country' and 'Parsing Judgement'.

Meanwhile, in the more serious 'populars', it was all much more to do with shake-ups and sortings-out. The *Daily Express* used the bottom left [*sic*] corner of page 2 to announce, 'English in schools set for a shake-up', which was expanded to 'A massive shake-up in the way English is taught was demanded yesterday in a Government report'. *Today* followed suit by revealing (on page 12), 'Teachers who bluff their way in English' and continuing with the deduction that 'poorly qualified teachers are to blame for children leaving school unable to read, write or even speak properly'. This problem seemed to have affected even the *Today* correspondent, who ended his piece by referring to the recommendation for schools to appoint a 'specially trained language consultant'. For the *Daily Mail* what mattered most was, 'Pupils to get reading and writing "targets"', following up with (again) 'A massive shake-up of English teaching in schools was urged yesterday'. But the *Mail* then pulled ahead of the *Express* and *Today* by giving details of the four main areas of the Kingman 'model'; a sub-heading, 'Committee says no to old-style grammar lessons'; and three neatly boxed summaries of the assessment targets at seven, eleven and sixteen, which *Today* had reduced to three items each, without saying so, and the *Express* had summarised in four general lines.

However, if anyone wanted to be better informed on the content and deliberations of Kingman the day after its publication (when even my local HMSO bookshop did not have a copy of the report itself), they would have to have been one of the two and half million who bought a quality newspaper. Within this sector of the press there were distinct differences in space allocation and detailed reporting.

Of these, the *Financial Times* was the briefest in coverage, stressing the right of all children to be able to use standard English and the Report's 'prime conclusion' that schools need to pay more attention to the standard version, while adding Kingman's qualification that speakers may be 'rightly proud' of regional pronunciation.

The *Guardian* and *The Times* provided only a little more material, the *Guardian* focusing on 'the most detailed recommendations', concerning the training of teachers, although it devoted over half its leader column to a discussion of the Report. *The Times* was more idiosyncratic, devoting the first part of its report to the statement on the next working party being handed to Sir John Kingman only minutes before the press conference. *The Times* interpreted this as a snub to the Kingman Committee and, for some reason, an indication that 'grammar lessons are to return to schools this year'.

As their front page priorities indicated, by far the fullest reports were to be found in the *Independent* and the *Daily Telegraph*. The *Independent* devoted a whole page to the Report, complete with a photograph of a pensive Sir John. The main article dealt with what children should learn, according to the Report, and others dealt with teacher union reaction, teacher training, full details of the model and the attainment targets, as well as the new working party and a delightfully indulgent article on the language lessons which can accrue from literary experience.

The *Daily Telegraph* allocated about two thirds of a page to the Report, including photographs of a more animated Sir John and the document itself. With a series of boxed headings, this page dealt with the task, the problem, targets, teacher training, recommendations, standard English, the model and a little nudge, using a Lynda Chalker reference, that we need to improve our performance in foreign languages too.

Space was more evenly allocated in the leader articles in the quality papers, with the main variation, predictably, being in the political stances they took. Here the *Telegraph* was least conciliatory, taking the fact that we needed Kingman to tell us this at all to be 'a measure of where we have got to'. Passing on from this rather exposed preposition, the *Telegraph* was fearful of the Report's 'equivocal' nature and that the 'experts' will now 'talk it to bits'.

The Times was similarly suspicious about Kingman already being 'denounced' by 'the education industry', although the paper's view was that the Report had fallen between the progressive Scylla and the Charybdis of 'nostalgia for ancient certainties'. Suspicion and apprehension continued through the leader which concluded that 'teachers should be made to learn, and teach, more basic grammar', without making it 'a fetish or a shibboleth', gleefully noting the 'not very lively' but standard English which was preferred by those who submitted evidence to the Committee.

The *Guardian* was more positively disposed towards the Report, memorably reaffirming that children brought up in an age of television 'are not as ready to sit in rows conjugating irregular verbs as their predecessors'. Here, too, there was talk of polarised arguments between 'contestants' who favour 'back to basics' and those favouring 'learning by osmosis', but the *Guardian* supported a compromise which recognised that 'the capacity to communicate has never been at a higher premium'.

The *Independent* provided the most informed and enthusiastic leader article because it was so impressed with the Committee's 'outstanding' work in recognising the 'teaching of English as a living language'. There was no doubt in this paper's mind that 'if ever a government document deserved to become the foundation for a national consensus, it is the Kingman Report'. But for those who felt that the *Independent* had impressed most in its range of reporting and its informed magnanimity, the *Daily Telegraph* had a special feature tucked away, a long 'inside story' by one of the Committee, P. J. Kavanagh. He was clearly older and wiser for the experience, never having quite recovered from a committee member suggesting that it was an impoverishment for pupils not to know about the English language and being told that it was an impoverishment for the committee member not to know Jamaican patois . . .

Kavanagh offered something unrivalled in the other papers, the sense of bewilderment at entering a professional world in which feelings ran so high, the whole-hearted admiration for the DES advisers and the secretary, who, hour after hour, were so discreet, quietly supportive and to the point when advice was needed. And Kavanagh is frank about the frustrations the Committee felt in trying to finalise the Report to make 'matter and manner coincide'.

Entering these newspaper pages is to enter more than different perspectives on the same world but to enter different worlds, defined not only by syntactical order and semantic priority. While any text, including this article, is a result of a selective and structured representation of the world, it is chastening to consider how many millions of people have been disadvantaged on this and many other occasions by the simple bias of omission.

Moreover, a look at the language of newspapers on occasions like this can have lessons for all of us. While we may sense differences of content, style and organisation, we may well need specialised concepts and linguistic terminology to describe and understand these differences more fully. Just as the Kingman

Report indicated the value of newspaper study, newspaper study can suggest the need for the kind of language repertoire which Kingman recommends.

6 Kingman on the Kingman Report

Doug Dennis

Introducing his report, in an address to the United Kingdom Reading Association Annual Conference at the University of Leicester in July 1988, Sir John Kingman said that he had wondered why he had been selected to chair the Committee and had been encouraged that others had asked the question too. However, as the work had progressed it had become clear to him why others might not have wanted the 'honour'.

He went on to explain that his approach to the task had been to follow the advice he had always given to examination students, that the first rule was to read the questions and the second rule was to read them again. He had, he said, examined with care the three terms of reference given to the Committee. The terms of reference had made it quite clear that his committee was not required to repeat the work of the Bullock Committee, but to address a much more circumscribed set of questions, and to report within a year.

The first term of reference, Sir John said, required his committee 'to recommend a model of the English language'. This had caused a lot of agonising, he explained, because the word 'model' turned out to have almost as many meanings as any word in the English language, some of which were clearly inappropriate. One of the inappropriate ones, he stated, was the idea that 'model' should be read as 'exemplar . . . something to be copied'. There was no expectation, he thought, that the terms of reference would lead to the production of a model of good English usage that children would have to copy as had been the case with the old copper plate handwriting books. Rather, that 'model' meant something wider, different from that.

At this point Sir John referred to his earlier comments on the rules of examinations and quoted his third rule, which was, 'If you cannot understand question 1 go to question 2'. His second term of reference had been 'to recommend the principles . . . how far and in what ways the model should be made explicit to pupils'. This, he said, gave a clue as to what the model was. It was something which might or might not be explicitly taught to children in our schools and it clearly had to do with the idea of teaching knowledge explicitly about the English language to children.

Sir John pointed out that consideration of this second term of reference had immediately brought into play two extreme views on the issue. There were those who had argued that all that was needed to improve the situation was a return to the pre-1960 style of English teaching, though he said that his committee had never actually met anyone who taught like that. Despite this lack of exponents, he said, there were certainly people who espoused the theory that this was what should be done. On the other hand there were those who had claimed that teaching anything about the English language was a mistake for a variety of reasons. Here again the Committee had found a difference between theory and practice, as many teachers who had adopted the view that they should not teach anything about language did, in fact, when they were observed in the classroom, teach quite a lot about language, whether or not they used the familiar technical terms.

He considered that these extreme views were caricatures to some extent, caricatures of practice if not of theory, and identified the great temptation to his committee in this situation of opposite extreme views. The temptation was to act as a sort of ACAS, taking valuable grains of truth from each case, splitting the difference and making an arbitration award which would annoy both sides equally and thus give some idea of impartiality. Sir John emphasised that this approach would have been quite wrong and that although his committee's recommendations were by definition between the extremes – there was nowhere else they could be – it had, in fact, gone back to some basic principles. It had tried to define the most sensible approach to the problem of teaching English language which, it hoped, would help teachers to do their job that much more effectively. Nevertheless, he felt that the term 'middle of the road' was quite right, although he preferred to think they were steering a broad channel in which there was a fair amount of choice for the master mariner to navigate his ship in the confidence that he would avoid the rocks on either side. He had chosen this analogy because he wanted to emphasise what his committee had tried to stress in its report: that they were not proposing the ultimate truth. They were not saying that this was 'the' way to do it, 'the' model of the English language. On the contrary, the Committee had tried to stress that almost all the questions raised needed a great deal more professional debate. They needed to be subjected to rigorous intellectual analysis, he said, and he would be very sorry if the report was not torn to shreds by the experts. But he would like it to be done in a reasonably informed, rigorous and sensible way.

The Committee was setting a broad channel within which the teaching profession, the experts on language and on child development could argue about the issues without feeling the need to take one of two extreme positions. In other words, the Committee's primary aim had been to raise the level of debate.

The Committee had been a very mixed and lively group incorporating some very experienced teachers, some distinguished academic experts on English language and language generally, some creative users of language such as writers and broadcasters, and some who had said things like 'Yes, but what happens in everyday life?'. The group had rarely reached agreement, said its Chairman, even on such matters as stopping for lunch or opening another bottle of wine, let alone the major issues facing them. He thought that they had regarded themselves as representatives, not of the teaching profession but of the community which the schools exist to serve. It had seemed right to them as a group that they should try to specify the challenge to the schools and what it was that English teaching was trying to do; what sort of achievement they would like their children to have; what sort of experiences and what sort of exposure. It had seemed that that was a fair thing for the group to do. It would have been a great mistake if the Committee had gone deeply into the 'how' and had tried to write a textbook on how to teach English. That was very much the problem of the teaching profession. The Committee had tried to give some examples of good practice because one of its functions had been to spread around its ideas and its observations.

In their visits to schools members had seen a lot of good practice. But they had not tried to answer in any detail the question, 'How do you teach English in schools?' Sir John Kingman stressed that that was very much a matter for the teaching profession, but that it was not a matter finally for the teaching profession to decide what should be taught. Schools existed because of the will of the community as a whole and it seemed right for the community to say something about what the schools should be aiming for. This he thought was part of the thinking behind some of the recent developments in education.

The Committee had had marvellous arguments about where to start, because wherever one chooses to start one can always go further back and always say, 'Why?', and go further and further back. Descartes had done this and he had ended up uncertain whether he existed let alone whether anyone else existed and eventually he cut the Gordian knot and said, 'Well, I've got to start somewhere: I think therefore I am'. Sir John thought that one possible interpretation of his illustration was that one should not try to go too far back. In trying to go back one got into questions which were, of their nature, unanswerable. The important thing when one was doing something that was practical politics rather than philosophy, was that one should try to find an agreed place to start.

The starting point on which the Committee agreed was, the Chairman thought, quite a simple one. They had expressed it in the covering letter to the Secretary of State which appeared at the beginning of their report as well as in the body of the report. The Committee said there, 'It must be a primary objective' – the Chairman thought some of them might have said '*the* primary objective' – 'It must be a primary objective of the education system to enable and encourage every child to use the English language to the fullest effect in speaking, writing, listening and reading'.

They had not found anyone who had disagreed with that although the meaning of the words in that simple sentence might well become controversial. What, for instance, did 'the fullest effect' mean? What did 'enable and encourage' mean? And when one started to unpack those words, of course, it led to consideration of more practical questions which were inevitably controversial.

Their starting point had been that an educational system which children left without that mastery of their own language was one which must have failed, however much mathematics or chemistry or physics studies or whatever had been pumped into the children. So a very fundamental role, in the Committee's view, of the educational system was the concept of mastery of the language. Difficult, ambiguous as it was, needing a great deal of explanation and unpacking, it had proved to be a useful starting point for what they had been trying to do.

Sir John apologised for the use of the word 'mastery', explaining that he had been denounced in a letter from a headmaster – or rather headteacher – for using a sexist word like 'mastery', but that he did not know of an alternative in English which did the job.

What was required was mastery, not just of standard English, but of all sorts of modes of the language. One of the elements of mastery was the ability to know what sort of English should be used on a particular occasion. Children, he said, need to come to understand from their teaching that there are different varieties of the language which should be used on different occasions; to be able to use English to the fullest effect means to have a mastery of some of those different modes. The Committee had encountered the libertarian argument which it had found an interesting one: 'If you tell children about Standard English, which they simply use to describe those conventions which are accepted at particular time and place as governing the English language in certain form and mode, it is limiting, or reducing their freedom'. But it had taken the view that telling the children about the 'conventions', such as the use of full-stops or the importance of a verb in a sentence, was important and helpful despite the arbitrary nature of the rules, because the child not confident in their use was the one who had been limited. Choice was available to the child who was confident, who could use standard English, who knew it was not appropriate in all circumstances. There might be occasions when the child wished to write in correct standard English or to speak in correct standard English, and there might be occasions when the child did not want to do so. The child then had the choice and, of course, had to live with the consequence of that choice, but that was where freedom started. The child who had been protected from the mysteries of standard English did not have that choice and did not have that freedom. Thus the Committee had turned the libertarian argument around on itself.

The same was true of some other arguments, too. It had been put to the Committee that by proposing to teach English to all children in a country like England they were trying to reject the other languages which exist in our society. The Committee had felt, on the contrary, that if there were children who had been deprived of the effective use of the English language because their home language or the language of their particular group, for example, was Welsh or Gujarati, then those children were condemned to being members of an underclass. There would be certain things in society to which they would not have access, their opportunities would be limited because they had not had access to the language which is the language of this country. There had been a number of arguments presented to the Committee which were rather like this, and it had come, therefore, to the idea of 'entitlement'. This was part of the underlying contract of the education system, that children were entitled to have this mastery of the English language if there was any way in which it could be given to them.

The third of the Committee's terms of reference had not been mentioned so far. In some ways it had been the most explicit because it had required, in effect, that the Committee draw up attainment targets for English language – not for the rest of the subject, literature and so on, but for language. Attainment targets were required for ages seven, eleven and sixteen and this had been both explicit and controversial. The Kingman Committee had been set up before the Task Group on Assessment and Testing but the TGAT Report had appeared during the Committee's deliberations and it had reported very much in line with the recommendations made by Professor Black and his colleagues. Before coming to the way in which the attainment targets had been expressed Sir John wanted to make the point that his committee would have understood its task more easily if it had read the terms of reference in the order 'three, two, one' rather than 'one, two, three'. He likened it to the classic detective story which was more fun if read from page 1 to page 200, but easier to understand if read from page 200 to page 1, because that was probably the way the author wrote it. He suspected that the same was true of the terms of reference.

The Committee had come to the attainment targets it actually produced a little late, because that was the 'how' and it had contented itself with illustrating the effect of its recommendations and trying to spread around a bit of good practice by talking about some of the good things that had been seen in schools. But in the end the question of 'how' had been related to the controversy which had given rise to argument. The controversy had been about explicit and implicit knowledge about language, or put in terms which would be familiar to teachers of every subject – the contrast between theory and practice. In any subject one might teach at any level one would teach by a mixture of telling the pupils and letting them find out for themselves, practising and developing their own skills. A good teacher would use the two in a very careful balance. As an example, Sir John suggested that the lecture he was delivering at that moment, was, on its own, a very cruel way of teaching any subject at any level. That sort of 'pure teaching' needed to be complemented with a great deal of practice on the part of the pupils, and part of the point of that practice would be that the pupils themselves discover things, learning things in a different way from simply 'taking them in'.

One of the most important skills of the good teacher was this balance between theory and practice, and he did not think it to be controversial in most subjects that there should be this balance. No one, he said, tried to teach Chemistry without practical classes but, equally, no one tried to teach Chemistry purely by giving sulphuric acid to the children and letting them get on with it. The problems attaching to that technique of teaching were fairly clear in Chemistry, but not so clear in other subjects. The balance had both to be there and to be used creatively. The concept was that one could 'tell' children, but one needed to choose the right moment to do the telling. The teacher needed to know that this was the very moment at which the children needed to know, for example, the second law of thermodynamics or what a verb is.

The Committee was, therefore, putting an enormous weight on the professional expertise of teachers. This had been done quite consciously. The Committee's confidence to do this had been given in large measure by their experience of looking around the schools and seeing what was going on. It had been clear that there were many good teachers who were perfectly capable of achieving a creative balance between theory and practice – between letting the children practise using the language in many different modes and developing their ability to do so, but at the crucial moment explaining to them why something was either working or not working in terms of their concepts about the structure and use of language.

The fact that the Committee was putting an enormous weight on the professional abilities of the teacher meant, of course, that the teaching profession as a whole needed to be properly prepared to meet this challenge. The Committee's most trenchant criticisms, Sir John feared, were directed at the institutions which taught teachers. That was where they did not find so much good practice, where the Committee had found English language to be seriously deficient. He was talking not only about colleges but also about universities. It was, he asserted, frankly a scandal that one could become a specialist teacher of English in a secondary school on the basis of a university degree which contained nothing about the language and was purely a degree in English Literature. The Committee had recommended that that scandal should be put right, and before the end of the century. For himself, Sir John did not think that the profession had that amount of time in which to make the change. Consequently the Committee was putting enormous weight on this. The worst possible reason teachers could have for not teaching language to the children in their charge was that they did not know about it themselves.

What then ought teachers to know? That was the content of 'the model'. The model the Committee had included was simply the description or representation of 'the English Language in use' which would serve as a basis for the way in which teachers should be prepared and the way in which they should think about their own job. It had been presented so that the report could be read whilst the pull-out schematic allowed the reader to view the model simultaneously. The model was, he said, something which would be unintelligible for most children in school, but it ought not to be unintelligible to specialist English teachers. Nor ought it to be unintelligible in so far as it was relevant to any sort of teaching, because every teacher in school, or indeed in university, was teaching English as well as the subject for which they were officially paid. So the model was simply the description of what the Committee thought teachers ought to know about English.

Examination would show that the model had a lot of familiar words in it. There were 'nouns' and 'verbs' and 'adjectives'. There were 'sentences' and 'paragraphs', 'commas' and 'semi-colons'. These were all familiar, so how did this differ from the sort of English that was taught in schools thirty years ago? It differed in two important ways: one of them was that the model was a description, not a set of rules. The old-fashioned method of teaching was cruel – to question why one ought not to split the infinitive would have been considered impertinent. Clearly this was an inadequate way in which to approach the language, which is living and has many rules, the status of which is complex and subtle. Very often an effective use of the language could be obtained by breaking the rules. This could be seen from the lengthy quotation in the report from *Bleak House*, in which the first long section had many sentences with no finite verbs at all in them, yet it was a very effective piece of writing. It was marvellously effective when the first verb appeared in the first sentence with a more conventional form. Very often the way to the effective use of language was to break the rules, but in doing so it was necessary to know what rules were being broken and by what method the effect was being achieved.

The Committee's model was not a prescriptive one, it was a descriptive model. The other thing it was not was a model which treated English as a branch of Latin. A lot of the classical grammatical concepts were rather difficult to understand without a knowledge of Latin because they referred to things which had almost disappeared. There was not really a lot of point in pretending that the English language was simply a rather down-market dialect of Latin. It never had been entirely that, and it was certainly not that today. English surely deserved to be treated as a language in its own right and that was what the model tried to do. Nor did the Committee claim that it was the last word on that subject. It expected, on the contrary, its model to be a basis for discussion and that teachers and others would talk about it in relation to its usefulness for teaching. There were, of course, other people who wanted models of language for other purposes – for example, those of the professional student of linguistics, or of a person trying to devise a computer program for translating between English and another language. This model was for the single problem of teaching all children as much as was possible so that they could master the English language in its various forms.

Once the model had been developed the next question had been the extent to which those concepts should appear as explicit items in a syllabus for examination, as explicit attainment targets. The Committee quite realised the danger that once it had been said that it was important that teachers should know what a verb was, then the question became: 'Should children know what a verb is, and if so, how should that be examined?'. These questions could not be ducked by saying that that was not what education was about, because it was known that, in the real world, the examinations had an enormous effect on what was taught and on the way it was taught. So there was a link between what happened in the classroom and how it was assessed. It was an extremely important one, one that they would neglect at their peril.

The Committee did not want examination papers saying, for example, 'Define an adjective' or 'Explain what a paragraph is'. That was not the object of the model in its report. It had tried to guard against that danger by a simple device which might or might not prove to have been effective. It had set out its attainment targets in two columns.

Targets which were about language in use and which would be tested implicitly by seeing whether children did in fact use them were in the left-hand column. The right-hand column was about understanding some of the concepts about the structure of grammar – not just grammar in its narrow sense of how sentences are put together, but a whole sweep from single letters right through to large connected passages. There were a lot of concepts in the right-hand column which it would like children to have the opportunity to understand. The testing of this, it thought, should be part of in-school assessment. In other words, teachers should ask themselves whether a specific child understands a particular concept – if the child does not, shouldn't they be doing something about it? Increased understanding would increase the child's mastery of the language in use. So the left and right columns were connected because the things which were in the left-hand column for examination would be tested by their use, and they were related to the concepts of the right-hand column which if applied by the child would aid that use.

This format might prove to be too subtle. However, he hoped not. It was, in fact, very important that the assessment system, however it evolved, should strengthen what the Committee was trying to do and not sabotage it, either by ignoring the structure of the language and saying that if children did not spell correctly it did not matter, or by turning the language into nice fodder for formal examination questions of the sort: 'Underline in red all the adjectives in the sentence'. Whether the Committee achieved that would remain to be seen.

The question very much in the minds of the Committee members was, of course, what would happen as a result of their report. Formally the Committee no longer existed; it had written and signed its report and handed it to the Secretary of State. The Secretary of State had said that he 'found the report interesting' which the Chairman interpreted as a compliment, though the real compliment would be what happened as a result.

One thing which would follow on naturally from the Committee's activities was the work of the group chaired by Professor Brian Cox – who had been a member of the Committee – which was to produce the National Curriculum in English. This was a wider job in the sense that it covered all the aspects of English in the curriculum. It was a narrower job because it was simply using the curriculum rather as they had been doing, trying to produce an underpinning for all the professional debate and professional decisions that had to be made. It had been made clear that the Cox group was expected to build upon the Kingman Report, and, as Brian Cox had been one of their enthusiastic members, the Chairman was confident that that would happen.

Professor Cox had a very difficult job, of course, since it was difficult enough to produce a curriculum in a nice, straightforward linear subject like Mathematics, but enormously more difficult to do in a subject like English which was not linear but had a highly complex structure. One of the things which had become very clear to the Committee as it worked was the way in which the four modes of English related to one another and the way in which other things which were not formally listed also related – for example, the fact that children who used unclear English were often thinking unclearly as well. The clarity of thought and the clarity of expression, whilst they were not equivalent, were strongly related. So Brian Cox had to build on what they had done, and also in the dimensions of literature and so on to produce the National Curriculum based on that work.

The Kingman Committee had also made some highly specific recommendations about the business of preparing the teacher. It was quite clear that a lot more time and effort in teacher training needed to be devoted to the English language at a general level; for specialist secondary teachers at another level; for non-specialist secondary teachers at another level again; and in some ways the most difficult level of all, for the primary teacher. All of this needed to be thought through. This, he hoped, was beginning to happen in the mysterious bodies which determine the future in colleges of higher education. He hoped that they might even begin to move the university English departments, but warned against exaggerating the power of the vice-chancellors in this respect. Of course, there was not time to wait for changes to take place in colleges and departments before achieving the changes in the teaching profession for which they had been arguing. For that reason a key role would have to be played by in-service training. It was thought rather shocking that English had not been made a priority subject for in-service training. The Committee understood that this would now be the case, and that financial resources were being made available in order to strengthen in-service training in particular to facilitate discussion about the issues which the Committee had raised in its report – discussion conducted in such a way that it would have a real effect on teaching in the classroom.

The Committtee's main objective had been more diffuse than that. It had been 'trying to raise the level of debate on these questions about the Teaching of English, so that they were not simply a matter of throwing half-truths around, a matter of slanging the other side'. Sir John Kingman hoped that they would hear less of the extreme positions, and that they would see the teaching flotilla advancing down the broad channel, some people to port and some to starboard, and some perhaps steaming rather faster, not too many lagging behind, or going aground, or running themselves against the jagged rocks on which certain sirens sat and sang their songs.

Time, he said, would tell!

7 The Kingman Report's Model of the English Language: Realities and Research

John Bald

The Kingman Committee's model of the English language is addressed to teachers rather than to pupils, and is intended to provide a core of knowledge about language which will inform and guide their work. It is presented in four parts, with one subdivision, as follows:

1. The Forms of the English Language
2.i Communication
2.ii Comprehension
3. Acquisition and Development
4. Historical and Geographical Variation

The model is illustrated by examples of work drawn from schools visited by committee members and by a bibliography of some 130 books and articles. The bibliography follows the subdivisions of the model, although the relationship of cited works to specific statements in the model is not specified and is often questionable. Although the Committee hopes that the model will be widely discussed, it recommends that it be adopted as presented.

Parts 1, 2 and 4 of the model concern aspects of language which have been susceptible to investigation by conventional research methods and about which there is a substantial body of evidence. This applies as much to the description of the elements of English as to historical and geographical variation, and the sections on communication and comprehension are both broad in scope and open-ended, giving weight to factors beyond literal meaning, such as inference, prior knowledge of a given topic and the attitudes of speaker and listener, reader and writer. Any controversy over the assertion in part 1 that combinations of linguistic forms yield meaningful language is removed if this is considered in the context provided by part 2.

Part 3, 'Acquisition and Development', which relates the model to the process of education, is less straightforward. The first section suggests that children 'gradually acquire the forms of language' described in part 1, and the second that they generally 'develop their ability to produce and understand' these in a broad range of contexts, both spoken and written. The processes are considered to overlap and to cover a range of aspects of language which appear at different rates. There is also some overlapping in the terminology itself, as the section on acquisition says that some aspects of the language 'develop' later than others. Part 3 as a whole comprises just four sentences, and is accompanied by a gloss of less than a page. This suggests that teachers should be able to distinguish between a 'normal' and an 'abnormal' pattern of development, the latter indicating a special need, and that one of the purposes of part 3 is to help them to distinguish between those aspects of language which are easy for a child at a given stage of development and those which are not.

The bibliography which accompanies part 3 includes the Bristol Child Development Study, Shirley Brice-Heath's *Ways with Words* (1983), Vygotsky's *Thought and Language* (1962), Tizard and Hughes's *Young Children Learning* (1984) and Margaret Donaldson's *Children's Minds* (1978). Each of these books shows that the process of language acquisition and development are more complex than the model and its gloss suggest.

Ways with Words describes the early language experience of three groups of children in the southern United States, one from managerial families and the other two respectively from black and white millworkers' families. The author identifies three distinct patterns of language use and development within the groups, and relates these to patterns of successes and failure in school. The children of the managerial group, whose parents miss no opportunity to involve them in conversation and read with them, are immersed in the ways of school from birth and are generally the most successful. The children from the white millworkers' families have a more restricted linguistic experience, with fewer books and less conscious language development on the part of their parents, while those from the black millworkers' families are expected to observe the adult scene rather than to participate in it and develop among themselves a vibrant oral culture which makes the early years of school appear boring and which does not contribute to literacy.

The Bristol study identified similar patterns in the early language experience and subsequent school careers of British children – one child had over 6,000 recorded encounters with books and stories before school, another none – while even Tizard and Hughes, who presented their research as a vindication of working-class upbringing, noted that the mothers from professional families in their sample encouraged children to ask questions 'beyond the here and now' and to express themselves clearly, while those from their working-class sample did not. Vygotsky described the specific requirements of literacy as an abstract mode of communication which did not repeat the developmental process of speech, while Margaret Donaldson brought this and cultural factors together in her investigation of the failure of the school system to engage large numbers of children in the most important dimensions of thought that it had to offer.

The different patterns of development revealed by this research are too widespread to be categorised as 'normal' and 'abnormal', and the cultural factors at the core do make it difficult to justify the committee's attribution of the enormous variations in the 'normal' pattern of development so unequivocally to ability.

Teachers face the problems posed by such cultural diversity every day, and will have little regard for general statements which are contradicted by their experience as well as by research. If a model of language acquisition and development is to be of any use to them, it must be based on analysis of the patterns and variations which are present in the real world, and must be sufficiently detailed to enable them to act on it.

References

Brice-Heath, S. (1983) *Ways with Words*. Cambridge University Press.

Donaldson, M. (1978) *Children's Minds*. Fontana, London.

Tizard, B. and Hughes, M. (1984) *Young Children Learning*. Fontana, London.

Vygotsky, L. S. (1962) *Thought and Language*. MIT Press, Cambridge, Mass.

8 The Kingman Report: A Model for Curriculum Planning or Instructional Design?

George Young

The Terms of Reference of the Kingman Committee

In 1987 the Kingman Committee was set up to develop a model of the English language as a basis for teacher training and professional discussion and to consider how far that model could provide a new basis for the teaching of English language in the school curriculum. In the early stages of its work proposals were made by the Secretary of State for the establishment of a national curriculum with programmes of study linked to targets of attainment to be statutorily prescribed for each of a number of key educational stages between the ages of 5 and 16. As English was one of the core subjects in these proposals their announcement could not be ignored by the Committee and the model that emerged from their deliberation was presented as a basis for the location of English within the order laid down by the Secretary of State, providing the conceptual framework for the attainment targets of the various competences which were to be the learning outcomes envisaged for the subject in the new curriculum. In fact, the intrusion by the Secretary of State must have changed somewhat the course of the Committee's discussions, bringing into the foreground of their thinking a clear and compelling criterion of the effectiveness of the model they were constructing. It had ultimately to provide an explicit framework for the principled specification of instructional objectives.

As a framework for instructional objectives the model produced had to connect the forms of languages to their use not only in the classroom but also in the functions of language in later, adult life which were seen as the ultimate goals determining the skills to be incorporated in the new curriculum. Indeed, the forms of language constitute only one of the four parts that form the primary structure of the model as it appears in the Report, the others being devoted to communication and comprehension, acquisition and development, and historical and geographical variation. In the Report the Committee is at pains to point out that it is not writing a linguistic textbook. A full description of the model would, it assures us, have inflated the final document, which is limited, therefore, in its description to a number of concepts illustrating broadly the abstract functions and instructional implications of each level of what is obviously presented as a stratified or hierarchical model, supported by a list of titles for further reference and clarification at each level.

The Kingman Model of Language Function

The constraints of both time and volume undoubtedly limited the degree of delicacy to which the Committee could go in clarifying the internal structure of the model in the main body of the Report. Where conceptual structure appears to be missing we can only assume that it has been left implicit to be extracted from the reading lists by the interested reader. Too much left implicit, however, leaves little ground for inference without resort to the lists and it is particularly incumbent on the authors to articulate key connecting concepts at critical points in the texts. An avowedly functional model must, after all, be descriptively adequate to the functions it purports to serve. When the model is stratified, the pressure for explicitness is greatest at the points of functional articulation between the various levels, particularly between Level 1, the forms of language, and Level 2, communication and comprehension, and between Part 4 of Level 1, 'phrase and sentence structure', and Part 5 'discourse structure'. Yet it is precisely here that there is inferential evidence, both from the description of the model and the illustration of its use in instructional practice, that a crucial functional concept was absent from the deliberations of the Committee. Let us call this concept by a term pioneered elsewhere, the 'functional sentence perspective' (Young 1989).

The Model of the Sentence

Under the heading 'phrase structure and sentence structure' one of the issues addressed by the Committee is 'what it is that is enclosed between a capital letter and a full stop' (p. 21). Certainly, any sentence must satisfy this graphological definition but it must also do much more than that, for the sentence is the unit of discourse which enables the clauses within it to operate as mechanisms of topicalisation and focus in writing. It has no clear analogue in speech where the utterance encloses a topic whose focus is more usually signalled by the contour and level of pitch. Its role in this respect is largely ignored in the Report which raises only two questions of sentence function, 'the relationship of sentence form to sentence function', and 'of sentence forms all of which "say the same thing"', which are left thereafter unexplored. The failure to produce a definition of the function of the sentence in discourse leaves Part 4 of Level 1, 'phrase and sentence structure', functionally unattached to Part 5, 'discourse structure', with its description of the major devices of coherence and cohesion. This gap in the model creates problems for instructional design. The role of the sentence renders its teaching the key instructional objective in any programme aimed at elucidating the very deep discoursal and syntactic differences between speech and writing. These differences themselves merit only a paragraph in the Report (para. 16, p. 25), a cursory treatment of an issue which should have been central to the concern of the Committee.

If a functional sentence perspective were implicit in the text, then the curriculum planner using the model could be usefully directed in pursuit of it to the reading list covering this section of the Report. However, the subsequent illustrations of the model in use suggest that the problem is much more than a failure of explication. Take, for example, the analysis offered of the strengths and weaknesses of the narrative by Ann, a seven-year-old girl:

Yesterday we went out for walk and we walked over some bridges and we saw some workmen and we went passed our house and Mrs Brown said that our garden was nice and we crossed the riverban and we went up mud lane and we saw sugar my partner was Joanne and when we came back it was playtime

'Ann', says the Committee, 'already has some grasp of sentence variation . . . As Ann progresses she will learn about the placing of full stops. She will see how events can be given different prominence by varying the sentence pattern . . .' (p. 34). Apart from some mention of errors in spelling and capitalisation, the comments in the text are clearly concerned with the role of the sentence. Yet the comments themselves are fragmentary and seem to be uninformed by an encompassing functional perspective. What is lacking is an appreciation that the root of Ann's problems lies in the absence of any understanding of the role of the sentence in writing. More particularly, she has yet to grasp the significance of the complex sentence, which embeds propositions from the context or the preceding text as a backdrop to a foreground which extends the discourse, pushes it forward, as it were, to its major informational focus, usually in a main clause at the end of the sentence. An older, more skilful writer, more attuned to the requirements of the sentence, might have rewritten the narrative somewhere along the following lines:

Yesterday we went out for a walk. We walked over some bridges and we saw some workmen. On our way past our house we saw Mrs Brown, who said that our garden was nice. Later, after crossing the river Bann, we went up Mud Lane, where we saw Sugar, and, when we came back, it was play-time. My partner was Joanne.

'Building on what the child already grasps', says the Report, 'the teacher will help her forward, perhaps initially by encouraging a second draft with some restructuring of her narrative' (p. 34), but without the assistance of an appropriate sentence perspective it is difficult to see how the teacher can enable such restructuring to occur.

The Model of Learning and Instruction

Whatever its weaknesses of design and conception, the model that emerges in the pages of the Report can only be judged ultimately by pragmatic criteria, as it was intended not to satisfy the canons of theory construction but to provide a useful framework for curriculum planning and instructional design. As such, the model must ultimately stand or fall by the credibility of its connections with the targets of attainment which, in part, set the context for the construction. Underlying this connection is another, deeper, more embedded model, a model of learning and instruction. The nature of this model can be inferred from the layout of the attainment targets in the text. The targets are placed in two parallel columns so as to represent two broad classifications of knowledge. On the left are placed performance criteria, overt, behavioural manifestations of tacit knowledge of the rules of grammar and socio-linguistic convention; on the right are examples of explicit knowledge of the relevant systems. The two types of target are laid out in sequences of parallel, matching pairs, suggesting a necessary correlation, not to say a causal relationship. As an example, row 5 of the columns consists of the juxtaposition of:

5. 'Use complex sentences appropriately to express complex relationships'.

5. 'Understand that different relationships may be expressed in sequences of simple sentences, simple co-ordinated sentences, and complex sentences containing subordinate clauses'.

The construction of the columns reflects the belief of the Committee 'that knowledge about language, made explicit when the pupil is ready can underpin and promote mastery as well' (p. 4). As an example, the Committee points to two common patterns of error in children's writing, omission of verbs and errors in pronoun usage, which can be helped, in the first case, by an introduction to the concept of the verb and its role in the sentence and, in the second, by some instruction in the general rules of pronominal reference. The knowledge taught is thus to be explicit knowledge of the rule systems but the method of instruction is to avoid the notorious declamatoriness of traditional grammar teaching by being both inductive, with the knowledge 'acquired mainly through an exploration of the language pupils use, rather than through exercises out of context' (p. 13), and eclectic, with the teacher deciding 'how much of that knowledge is made explicit to a pupil or class at a given moment, and how it might be done' (p. 37). In the classroom eclecticism tends to follow in the wake of the inductive method; children progress at very different rates and provide somewhat diverse opportunities for teaching based upon their own texts. To allow the teacher freedom to pursue this method, the Committee departs from the textbook rules of practice for the formulation of objectives in their description of the targets of explicit knowledge. These are expressed as targets of 'understanding' as opposed to those of 'use' or 'writing' which are the most common specifications of the performance column.

In constructing the model as a framework for both curriculum planning and instructional design the Committee raises two issues of learning and instruction which it is incumbent upon it to confront on other than a purely intuitive basis. Does explicit knowledge of the rule system facilitate development in performance? Is the inductive/eclectic approach advocated more effective in attaining the objectives of the Report than other more wholly expository and deductive modes of instruction? The affirmative response of the Committee to the first of these questions presupposes a transfer of learning between two very different universes of behaviour. Writing and speech are motor activities involving cognitive operations of a synthesising and creative kind. In contrast, the acquisition of explicit knowledge of the rule systems they exploit is essentially a process of segmentation and decomposition into concepts of a high level of abstraction. Previous research has tended to test the attainment of the concepts rather than the effectiveness of their transfer to other motor skills. The possibility of transfer between the two universes of behaviour has never been demonsrated. In the Report the gap is filled by impressionistic accounts of classroom practice evidently chosen because they display some application of explicit knowledge although it is difficult to see why in these instances linguistically less informed instruction in behavioural skills would be any less effective. Clearly this is an area for research. In the absence of such work the assumptions that underlie the application of the model must remain little more than articles of faith.

The validity of the inductive/eclectic method advocated in the Report turns upon the extent to which it can accommodate two axioms of learning theory. The first of these is that, at least in the early stages, concepts to be learned must have identifiably empirical referents. The second is that they must also have some potential linkage to the pre-existing cognitive structure of the learner. The progression from primary abstractions with immediate referents to secondary, higher-order concepts is presumably the aim behind the Committee's espousal of the use of the child's own text as a basis for teaching. Here the difficulties encountered are less conceptual than practical. Sadly, says the Report, the 1978 HMI survey

'Primary Education in England' found that 'in only about a third of classes were samples of children's work regularly used to monitor this progress' and that 'in fewer than half of the classes was children's own written work used as a basis for teaching spelling, syntax, sentence structure or style' (p. 50). The justification for the text-centred method lies in the popular assumption among learning theorists that the single most important factor influencing learning is what the learner already knows; however, the application of this assumption to the field of language development serves only to return us once more to the question of the nature of the connection between the two types of knowledge outlined in the Report. The child does have linguistic knowledge of a kind but it is the tacit knowledge of the rule system that forms the competence which is ultimately realised in performance. Whether or not such implicit knowledge can provide a conceptual basis in performance for the construction of a system of explicit knowledge of the rules that underlie it is a question only ultimately resolvable by empirical research. Pending the arrival of such work, the case *a fortiori* of the inductive method would probably lie in the teaching of the closed system of the language.

Models of Learning and Language Systems

Closed systems are those whose membership remains relatively stable over time. They tend to be smaller than the more fluid open systems and functionally more homogeneous and, by virtue of these limitations, easier to isolate and analyse without implicating a multitude of other systems. A good example is the pronoun system, a closed system consisting of a small number of items united in expressing the kind of pronominal cross-reference which is essential for the cohesion of discourse. It is significant that it is this system which is chosen by the Committee as one of the areas to illustrate their inductive and eclectic method. The other area they choose is more problematic. This is the verb phrase. The verb was probably chosen because of its pivotal function in the clause but this very centrality is what makes it a difficult concept to acquire in isolation. The function of the verb phrase cannot easily be taught without reference to the noun phrase and, indeed, both phrase and clause structure in general, for 'word', 'phrase', and 'clause' are the terms of a hierarchy of constituent concepts which even postgraduate students, coming fresh to linguistics, find difficult to grasp without fairly extensive explicit teaching.

Nowhere in the Report is there a clue for teachers of how to proceed eclectically without an agreed-upon theoretical framework in which such conceptual connections have been made explicit. The Committee makes much of the concept of 'readiness' but for this to be exploited with diagnostic skill the classroom teacher would have to have a fully explicit model of language as well as a knowledge of norms of language development. Neither of these figures at the moment in pre- or in-service training and their incorporation would bespeak a much greater allocation of resources to language training than that advocated in the Report.

Curriculum Planning and Instructional Design

In any exercise of the kind undertaken by the Kingman Committee it is essential to separate curricular issues from questions of instructional design. Curriculum design requires, first, the analysis of the concepts in a field of knowledge and, second, detailed consideration of the key relations between them. Failure to meet these requirements has been a traditional source of weakness and confusion in curriculum planning. The first task of instructional design is to explore the relationship between this conceptual structure and the linking concepts, if any, in the learner's cognitive structure. The nature of the relationship uncovered will determine the path of instructional objectives through the conceptual structure of the curriculum, whether inductive or deductive, implicit or explicit, linear or cyclical, top–down or bottom–upwards and so forth. The pathways chosen are contingent and cannot change the essential neutrality of instructional programmes with respect to the conceptual structure of the curriculum. This the Committee failed to recognise. In their report the model they embrace is left loose and inexplicit in the belief, on their own admission, that this gives greater freedom of instructional manoeuvre. The reverse is almost certainly the case. A more precise and detailed formulation of the model would have better focused the profession on the question of how best to teach a complex conceptual structure at different ages and levels of ability and attainment. From this exercise a greater range of alternative solutions would have come. As it is, the freedom of the teacher to intervene effectively in the language development of the child can only be diminished by the recommendations of a report irrevocably flawed by the failure to separate curriculum planning from instructional design.

References

Department of Education and Science (1988) *Report of the Committee of Inquiry into the Teaching of English Language* (The Kingman Report). HMSO, London.

Young, G. (1989) 'Speech and writing: the development of a model with a functional sentence perspective', in Hunter-Carsch, M. *The Art of Reading*. Blackwell Education, Oxford.

9 Kingman in the Classroom: Practical Ideas for Developing Language Awareness

Sue Palmer and Peter Brinton

With the publication of the Kingman Report in April 1988, a long period of uncertainty for teachers on the subject of English language teaching has, we hope, come to an end. Kingman supported neither the 'back to basics' brigade with their calls for a return to 'old-fashioned grammar lessons', nor the extremists of the opposite camp who would wish to restrict children's access to information about language lest it impede their creativity. Instead the Committee took the reasonable middle line that 'there is no reason why the subject of language should not be discussed like any other', and that knowledge about the way language works should be made available to pupils throughout their education.

During the three years preceding the Kingman Report, we were involved in devising a course in 'language awareness' for primary school pupils, and at the 1987 UKRA Conference we put forward a case for language teaching very similar to that suggested in the Kingman Report. We argued that to restrict pupils' access to knowledge about the way language works, and to the technical terms with which one can discuss it, is deleterious not only to their developing literacy skills but to their educational progress as a whole.

We suggested that the reasons for many teachers' distaste for teaching about language in the post-Plowden years may have been related more to typical pre-Plowden teaching methods (the famous 'old-fashioned grammar lessons') than to any real disagreement with the subject matter. The way to overcome this distaste is, of

All the activities in this chapter are taken from Books 1–4 of *Mind your Language* by Sue Palmer and Peter Brinton (Oliver and Boyd, 1988). The figure on p.86 is reproduced by permission of Oliver and Boyd.

course, to devise better, more exciting and more effective teaching methods.

We wondered also whether the aversion to language teaching over the last twenty years was, perhaps, connected with various emotional reactions to the term 'grammar', which in the '60s and '70s was generally associated with traditional educational methods, with attention to insignificant detail at the expense of a wider view ('grammatical points'), and with selectivity and elitism in education ('grammar schools'). Such unfavourable associations can, of course, be removed by a change in terminology and a wider field of reference. (Kingman took this course by referring to 'knowledge about language'; we preferred 'language awareness'.)

Beyond these associations, linguistic and educational, we could see no viable reason why English teachers should wish to restrict their pupils' access to the metalanguage of their subject than should teachers in any other area of the curriculum. Indeed, if in other curriculum areas, such as Mathematics, it had become axiomatic that children should learn correct terminology at the earliest opportunity, why should such access to vocabulary be denied in English, which is the basic tool for all children's learning?

As practising teachers, however, we were in full agreement with Kingman that teachers should not concentrate on teaching about language to the detriment of teaching language itself. We too argued that 'the best way to learn to write in the English language is to write in the English language, for a variety of purposes and audiences and in a meaningful motivating context' and that knowledge about language should be taught 'as an aid to this purposeful language work (and not as an end in itself)'.

We did, however, suggest that some teaching was essential. How would pupils otherwise come to share with their teacher the vocabulary of metalinguistic terms and grammatical concepts which would enable them to discuss and restructure their work? Thus we cannot entirely agree with Kingman that 'knowledge about language is not a separate component of the primary or secondary curriculum . . ., but should inform children's talking, writing, reading and listening in the classroom'. We believe that the Committee (like subsequent committees) was a little unrealistic about what can be achieved 'incidentally' in the classroom.

In the primary stages at least, some time must be devoted to ensuring that children know the meaning of linguistic terminology and some of the rules which underlie the system. If teachers rely on 'incidental teaching' techniques only (letting individual children in on the secret of, for instance, what a noun is, only if it happens to crop up in conversation), pupils' knowledge would be patchy in the extreme. Teaching about language need not, however, mean the 'old-fashioned grammar exercises' which Kingman (and all post-Plowden educationists) so rightly eschew.

Language Awareness Activities

For many years now, Mathematics teaching has exploited what is known about young children's learning process to very good effect. Concrete materials, activity methods, opportunities for children to 'discover' mathematical concepts for themselves are now accepted parts of practically every primary school's Mathematics curriculum. There seems no reason why these same successful methods should not also be applied to language teaching. Language, like mathematics, is a mass of abstract concepts, but the raw material – words – is as concrete as the raw material of maths. Children can become actively involved with words – picking them up and looking at them, playing with them, rearranging them, discovering interrelationships between them – just as productively as they can with numbers.

Indeed, as the Kingman Report points out, games and word-play are the natural means by which children explore language for themselves: 'children in particular are fascinated by word-games – by puns, backslang, tongue-twisters, conundrums, double meanings, anagrams, palindromes, etymologies and "secret" languages'. It seems both educationally and developmentally acceptable, therefore, to provide pupils with language experiences which include language games, puzzles and activities which will take over where their own explorations leave off, and furnish them with a language vocabulary and an appreciation of how language works.

Such activities, and the guided discussion about language which should accompany them, cannot practically be carried out on an 'incidental' basis, when a particular language point arises in discussion with an individual child. They are best pursued as class activities, a separate part of the language curriculum, through which all children will gain familiarity with vocabulary and concepts.

When playing with language, of course, different children will appreciate it at different levels: some may have little grasp of any linguistic implication, but just enjoy the 'game' aspect; others may begin to make the leap from an intuitive understanding of the language involved to an awareness of it as a language form; others, with growing awareness of linguistic implications, may be consolidating their understanding of metalinguistic terms and concepts and becoming ready to apply this understanding in their own written work. The teacher will then be in a position to intervene 'incidentally' with particular children or groups at the appropriate point in their writing development, without having to clutter the moment with impromptu language lessons – the 'language awareness' will already be there.

In the list of objectives for 11-year-olds given by Kingman, for example, it is clear that pupils will benefit from knowing the names of the principal parts of speech – nouns, verbs, adjectives, adverbs, pronouns. They are also expected to be familiar with the main elements of English punctuation and the ways in which these correspond with the intonation patterns of speech. Sections 4a–d require an appreciation of the structure of a simple sentence and the ways in which it can be transformed. Section 13 expects an appreciation of the variety of spoken dialects in English and their relationship with Standard English.

We include here some examples of the sort of games and activities with can be used as part of a primary 'linguistic awareness course' to introduce pupils to and familiarise them with these concepts.

Parts of Speech

In the 'traditional grammar lesson' the name of a particular part of speech would be given by the teacher along with a definition ('A noun is a naming word') and a number of examples. Pupils would then generally be required to work through exercises about nouns – copying them, underlining them, listing them, and so on. This was, of course, for most children an entirely passive and meaningless activity. And yet most children of eight or so already have an implicit understanding of what a noun is – if stimulated to take interest in the subject, they are able to produce endless examples of nouns for themselves. They cannot usually explain what it is the words have in common, but they are usually prepared to spend some time puzzling about this. Teaching methods can be devised to build on children's implicit knowledge about the language we speak.

For example, we used a story about a visitor from another planet who had a very limited vocabulary. At the end of the story, children were invited to play 'The Nodrog Game' (Figure 9.1): the teacher played the part of Nodrog and responded with either recognition or bewilderment to words suggested by the class. Words that Nodrog understood were written on the blackboard, others ignored. Once a group of children had begun to produce only nouns for Nodrog's delectation, they were told that these sorts of word had a special name. Other games such as 'Alphabetical Nouns' were introduced. Only after pupils had become quite familiar with the particular class of words did we give a definition.

Other parts of speech can be practised in the same way. Adjectives are needed for 'The Minister's Cat' (the Victorian parlour game), there are many mime/drama games you can devise to practice verbs, and most teachers already know 'The Adverb

What do the words that Nodrog understands have in common?

The words that Nodrog understands are called nouns.

Figure 9.1

Game', where pupils are asked to perform specific actions 'in the manner of the adverb' they have secretly chosen ('slowly', 'quietly', 'drunkenly'), while the rest of the group try to guess the adverb.

Punctuation

The relationship between punctuation and speech may best be established through reading aloud. Here again, drama can be helpful. The enaction of playlets written in 'gobbledy-gook' but with adequate punctuation can give a powerful indication of the extent to which our appreciation of language depends on intonation and chunking. And untangling other people's errors is often a useful stimulus to understanding. A pupil may not be able to tell you why a full stop should go in a particular place, but he can usually tell you why it shouldn't.

Sentence Construction

Sentence construction provides the opportunity for lots of 'manipulative activities' – picking words up and putting them together to make sense (or nonsense!). The 'Concoct a Sentence' game gives practice in subject–verb agreement, and the age-old format of 'Consequences' can be revamped to involve the creation of SVO sentences with adverbials thrown in if you like!

Dialect and Standard English

Children usually delight in other people's dialect and its divergence from the standard form, and this is a rich field for discussion. They can also soon be interested in their own dialect and those of people close to them, and 'spoken language projects' using tape-recorders to capture the richness of local dialects are often very successful. Investigation of slang, their own and other generations', is a particularly stimulating activity.

We hope we have conveyed through these examples that the study of language can be conducted without recourse to 'old-fashioned grammar lessons' – that, indeed, it can be enormous fun. Many of the games we include here were actually devised originally for party entertainment, proving that a spontaneous interest in language is, of course, natural in human beings. The good teacher is the one who is able to tap and direct children's natural interests, making learning fun and fun learning. And through this sort of game, puzzle, talk and activity children can acquire all the specialised vocabulary and knowledge they require to develop their own understanding and use of language throughout the curriculum.

10 Diversity and Common Ground in Language Awareness

Peter Garrett and Carl James

The term 'language awareness' (LA) slips so easily off the tongues, pens and printers nowadays, and in such a wide range of contexts, that one feels it more and more necessary to stop and consider what people mean when they use the term. What are the different understandings people have of LA? It was this question that led to the Seminar on Language Awareness at University College of North Wales, Bangor, in April 1989, organised for and through the British Association for Applied Linguistics (BAAL).

Readers may well find themselves reacting at this point. 'What do you mean, "different understandings"? I know what I mean, and everyone else I work with uses the term to mean the same as I do.' Within the British educational system, indeed, there has grown up a British Language Awareness Movement, and most will doubtless understand LA in terms of what it means there.

The EFL Field

Consider, though, where an EFL teacher, perhaps not so familiar with what is happening in the mainstream of British education, might come across the term, and how s/he might see LA. For example, in their EFL teacher training course, Hubbard et al. (1983) include a section called 'Language Awareness' (p. 163). This comes in their chapter entitled 'Planning and Preparation', which 'aims to help the teacher to teach' (p. 155). No explanation of the term is provided, and the activities set out under the LA rubric are restricted mainly to highlighting the often asymmetrical relationships between forms and functions.

On a somewhat different note, Gairns and Redman (1986) open their teachers' guide to teaching and learning vocabulary with a chapter headed 'Language Awareness Activities'. These activities 'focus on typical problems learners encounter when acquiring vocabulary, as well as on certain pedagogical questions' (p. 3). Teachers are invited to carry out activities which draw their attention to, for instance, cognates, word formation, and the question of whether to teach vocabulary in semantic or formal groupings.

In addition, there is the flourishing 'humanistic' sector of TEFL seen, for example, in the materials produced by Frank and Rinvolucri (1983) and Rinvolucri (1984). Their 'awareness activities' engage learners in practising grammar whilst expressing things about themselves or people who are significant to them. Here, then, LA is implicitly defined as grammar practice with a meaning-focused and personalised character.

EFL teachers curious enough to delve deeper into the field of Applied Linguistics might also come across Rutherford's (1987) LA, or 'consciousness-raising' (CR). Here the focus is also on grammar in second and foreign language learning. Rutherford's CR entails the controlled and principled supply of new language data to the language learner. The learner's attention is directed at specific features of the language in order to help the learner formulate and test hypotheses about the target language (p. 18).

Elsewhere in the EFL literature, other meanings surface. Interestingly, for example, LA for Golebiowska (1984) appears to mean somehow making foreign language learners more aware of the magnitude of the language learners' task, thereby increasing the motivation of 'those who know it all' (p. 274). Learners are to be made aware 'that the more proficient one is, the more fascinating this [foreign language] study can be' (p. 278).

Working within TEFL, then, one is likely to come away with either quite a range of understandings or a rather fuzzy idea of what LA is. As we shall see later, outside the British Language Awareness Movement, it is not only within the broad and thriving field of TEFL that LA is also found; the participants from overseas at the Bangor Seminar delivered some highly stimulating work in other areas also falling under the heading 'Language Awareness'.

The British Language Awareness Movement

Much of the discussion of language awareness in the UK owes a great deal to the pioneering work of Hawkins (1981, 1984). In response to the disastrous records regarding adult illiteracy and the low achievement in foreign language learning in Britain, Hawkins argued for the implementation of LA ('awareness of language', in fact, rather than 'language awareness') in terms of whole pro-grammes of study. These would ameliorate the situation in a number of ways: by bridging and transition from primary to secondary education language work, bringing together the different fields of language education (English, Modern Languages, ESL for ethnic minority pupils, etc.), facilitating discussion of linguistic diversity (on the assumption that this would decrease prejudice), and developing listening skills (for better foreign language study), as well as confidence and interest in reading and writing. Here, then, we have a movement seeking to establish programmes of study in the British educational system. To a large extent, it seems that this LA has been implicitly defined by its goals and content. Donmall (1985), however, bravely offers this explicit definition: 'Language Awareness is a person's sensitivity to and conscious awareness of the nature of language and its role in human life' (p. 7).

This is a definition with considerable breadth. And indeed, not only alongside, but even within the British LA movement, there is considerable diversity in the realisations of LA. This is clearly reflected in the wide range of the seminar papers, which are outlined below.

The Bangor Seminar

Most of the papers given at the Bangor Seminar related to this broad and diverse field of British LA, albeit dealing with rather different areas within it. Some were directed more at programmes and materials. Anderson provided a rationale for a cross-curricular approach to LA in secondary schools, and showed how this had worked at The Joan Roan School in London. Donmall considered how LA work might help to realise the objectives associated with the teaching and learning of modern foreign languages. Heap reported on his evaluation of the effectiveness of an LA course in

Wigan; an important contribution in the sadly and badly neglected area of assessment (see below). Little and Singleton, drawing on their experience with the 'Authentik' materials produced at Trinity College, Dublin, focused on the question of how the analytic and automatised dimensions of foreign language learner competence can best be promoted: information about the foreign language, it was argued, can not only foster certain skills, strategies and processes, but also increase the comprehensibility of foreign language input. Tinkel described the LA syllabus, course and methodology developed over a number of years for the sixth form at The Oratory School.

Others focused more on the teachers, and their views and expectations. Merchant based his paper on the view that, if teachers are being asked to respond positively to linguistic diversity, it is essential that we first find out what they understand by the term. His questionnaire revealed an interesting range of responses from primary school teachers. While Mitchell and Hooper gave a preliminary report on their investigation of teachers' opinions regarding the place of explicit discussion about language in language teaching, and how it might affect language development in children, Brumfit set out some ideas for building linguistic understanding into teacher attention to teaching methodology, arguing, on the basis of his work at Christ Church College, Canterbury, that LA may be particularly appropriate in teacher education for non-native teachers.

Clark and Ivanic provided another extension into tertiary education with their workshop demonstrating how LA can and should be integrated into a purposeful context of language use; in this case, academic writing for study skills students at Lancaster. Hedge and Gosden tackled the role of LA in academic writing, reading and study skills for overseas students at Liverpool. Their programme aims to make learners aware of those existing and developing cognitive strategies which they employ in a range of reading and writing tasks in English. Scholfield reported on his use of computer software at Bangor to prompt undergraduates and teachers on MA degrees to think about the English language, stressing the importance of monitoring the discussion stimulated by the computer. Sylvester gave an account of the gradual transition from a Linguistics Foundation course to an LA-type linguistics programme on the Area Studies degrees at Portsmouth Polytechnic.

To add to the diversity above, somewhat different perspectives on LA appeared in papers by three overseas contributors, Chryshochoos, Masny, and Nicholas. Chryshochoos, with foreign language learners' needs and syllabus design in mind, looked at learners' awareness of themselves in the learning process: their difficulties in language use, and of what constitutes effective language learning. Masny, seeing LA as 'individuals' ability to reflect on and match intuitively spoken and written utterances with their knowledge of the language', reported on her Canadian study of what second language learners' language (acceptability) judgements are based on at various stages of language proficiency. Nicholas studied how different forms of language awareness offer new criteria for distinguishing between first and second language acquisition, and between younger and older child second language acquisition.

Why the Diversity?

We have so far encountered quite a variety of meanings for LA. Yet in none of them does the use of the term 'language awareness' seem odd or inappropriate. The expression itself, it seems, is conveniently comprehensive; yet at worst it is also inherently imprecise. Let us take each of the two words in turn, starting with 'awareness'. What is it that we become aware of? Presumably, 'knowledge' of various types; information in the broadest sense. Knowledge external to us, that we now become aware of; or knowledge that we already possess, but did not realise we possessed. The former and the latter respectively call to mind Krashen's (e.g. 1981) 'learning' and 'acquisition' dichotomy, with the latter implying that we can learn about what we have acquired.

Language Awareness

Some LA work (e.g. see above: Sylvester; Tinkel) is organised in groups sharing a mother tongue, and aims to make students more aware (by which is meant 'conscious'), through exploration and discovery, of the intuitions they have about 'their' language. Implicit knowledge becomes explicit knowledge. LA is a means bridging the 'consciousness gap' within the individual. By guiding the learner's attention to specific language features, these are (hopefully) 'raised to consciousness', rather as in Rutherford's (1987) CR, but with the focus here on the first language.

In contrast, other LA work takes place with many learners who do not share a mother tongue. Here, then, efforts are made not only to make pupils aware of their own implicit knowledge of their first language, but also of each other's explicit knowledge. There is a concentration on language diversity, on the differences and similarities in all the languages present in the LA group. This latter, then (the LA of the multilingual and multicultural classrooms), is a means of bridging a 'knowledge gap', or even an 'information gap'. Although such gaps may become divisive 'conceptual gaps', and even barriers between pupils in the same class, LA taps the brighter side, since such gaps can also be exploited by the resourceful teacher as natural contexts for talking about language. Here, consciousness-raising occurs in the rather different sense of increasing (raising) the overall amount of conscious knowledge in each individual through new and explicit input.

In addition, there is the LA work aimed more at foreign language learners. By making learners more conscious of their mother tongue intuitions, of the specific relations (contrasts and similarities) between their mother tongue and the foreign language, and of how languages in general work, ways may be found to increase their explicit knowledge of the workings of the foreign language, and their motivation to learn it.

Language *Awareness*

The word 'language' can, of course, be used in a generic sense (languages across the board) or a specific sense (a particular language, such as French, or perhaps even the language of science, or the language of narrative). Notice how the word 'language' in Hawkins's term 'awareness of language' has a somewhat less broad range of meaning.

In the ingredients of an LA programme, the proportions of implicit knowledge raised to consciousness on the one hand and new explicit knowledge (= input) on the other will reflect which of these meanings is dominant. 'Multicultural LA' will tend to be 'generic LA', with each pupil finding far more new explicit input than implicit knowledge raised to consciousness. First language LA will tend to be 'specific LA', and will contain relatively more activities designed to raise implicit knowledge to consciousness. The language of narrative? One could envisage this being taught in a variety of contexts, such as the language of English narrative, or the language of a foreign language narrative. The language of narrative in two or several languages could be compared and contrasted in a bilingual or multilingual classroom.

Linguistic Diversity

In addition, the word 'language' has a modifying function. What is the difference, for example, between 'language diversity' and 'linguistic diversity'? Is there then a distinction to be made between 'language awareness' and 'linguistic awareness'? Masny, coming at LA from the psychology of learning, employs the latter term.

Common Ground

Underlying Currents

In the introduction to his BAAL seminar paper, Nicholas picks up on the number of different definitions of LA. In contrast to his own work in Australia, LA in Britain is an educational movement aiming at making pupils more conscious of the nature of language. Increased conscious reflection and illuminating talk on language by students and teachers is said to lead to improved language use and better overall education. Awareness, it is believed, leads to development. To quote from the Kingman Report (DES, 1988), for example: 'We believe [sic] that with English as a subject, pupils need to have their attention drawn to what they are doing and why they are doing it because this is helpful to the development of their language ability' (p. 13).

For Nicholas, however, development may influence the 'awareness' learners have of language quite independently of conscious reflection on language. Learners, he argues, may be aware of language without being able to articulate their awareness explicitly.

Nicholas regards these two views of LA as being complementary rather than conflicting. Their common ground is awareness and development, with conscious reflection being the point of difference. In British LA, because it is an educational movement, the role of conscious reflection is essential; in giving an account of aspects of language development, its role is variable.

Underlying Questions

Nicholas's work in LA raises the crucial question of what the precise relationship is between knowledge and awareness. We can 'know' something without being conscious of it or able to talk about it (see, for example, Sharwood Smith, 1981, p. 164). But can we be aware of something without being conscious of it, if not being able to talk about it? It is interesting that Mitchell and Hooper's paper talks about teachers' 'knowledge about language'. Similarly, Chandler, Robinson and Noyes (1988) appear to be making a distinction between linguistic knowledge and awareness in their study of students training to be primary teachers.

Does it Work?

In so far as LA is seen in terms of its applications in various fields and at various levels of education, we have intimated above, in relation to Heap's paper, that we feel it is important to stress the urgent need for the evaluation of its effectiveness. To what extent do LA programmes achieve their objectives? If they don't, why don't they? If they do, why do they? The Kingman Report, after all, is based more on belief in than evidence of the effectiveness of such work (see above quotation). And Crystal (1988, p. 9), writing specifically about grammar, wisely reminds us that improved awareness cannot guarantee better practice. 'Even after a course on car mechanics, we can still drive carelessly.'

References

Anderson, J. (forthcoming) 'The potential of language awareness as a focus for cross-curricular work in the secondary school' in *Proceedings of the British Association for Applied Linguistics Seminar on Language Awareness*. Longman, London.

Brumfit, C. (forthcoming) 'Language awareness in teacher education' in *Proceedings of the British Association for Applied Linguistics Seminar on Language Awareness*. Longman, London.

Chandler, P., Robinson, W. P. and Noyes, P. (1988) 'The level of linguistic knowledge and awareness amongst students training to be primary teachers.' *Language and Education*, 2 (161–73).

Chryshochoos, N. (forthcoming) 'Awareness of what?' in *Proceedings of the British Association for Applied Linguistics Seminar on Language Awareness*. Longman, London.

Clark, R. and Ivanic, R. (forthcoming) 'Consciousness-raising about the writing process' in *Proceedings of the British Association for Applied Linguistics Seminar on Language Awareness*. Longman, London.

Crystal, D. (1988) *Rediscover Grammar*. Longman, London.

Department of Education and Science (1988) *Report of the Committee of Inquiry into the Teaching of English Language* (The Kingman Report). HMSO, London.

Donmall, B. G. (ed.) (1985) *Language Awareness*. NCLE Papers and Reports, no. 6, CILT, London.

Donmall, B. G. (forthcoming) 'Language awareness in relation to the teaching and learning of modern foreign languages: an investigation with specific reference to pre-GCSE teaching in UK secondary schools' in *Proceedings of the British Association for Applied Linguistics Seminar on Language Awareness*. Longman, London.

Frank, C. and Rinvolucri, M. (1983) *Grammar in Action*. Pergamon, Oxford.

Gairns, R. and Redman, S. (1986) *Working with Words*. CUP, Cambridge.

Golebiowska, A. (1984) 'Motivating those who know it all.' *English Language Teaching Journal*, 38 (274–8).

Hawkins, E. (1981) *Modern Languages in the Curriculum*. CUP, Cambridge.

Hawkins, E. (1984) *Awareness of Language: An Introduction*. CUP, Cambridge.

Heap, B. (forthcoming) 'Evaluation of the effectiveness of an LA course' in *Proceedings of the British Association for Applied Linguistics Seminar on Language Awareness*. Longman, London.

Hedge, N. and Gosden, H. (forthcoming) 'Language awareness and EAP courses' in *Proceedings of the British Association for Applied Linguistics Seminar on Language Awareness*. Longman, London.

Hubbard, P., Jones, H., Thornton, B. and Wheeler, R. (1983) *A Training Course for TEFL*. OUP, Oxford.

Krashen, S. (1981) *Second Language Acquisition and Second Language Learning*. Pergamon, Oxford.

Little, D. and Singleton, D. (forthcoming) 'Language awareness, pedagogical grammar and foreign language learning: some practical proposals' in *Proceedings of the British Association for Applied Linguistics Seminar on Language Awareness*. Longman, London.

Masny, D. (forthcoming) 'Language learning and linguistic awareness: the relationship between proficiency and acceptability judgements in LA' in *Proceedings of the British Association for Applied Linguistics Seminar on Language Awareness*. Longman, London.

Merchant, G. (forthcoming) 'Linguistic diversity and language awareness' in *Proceedings of the British Association for Applied Linguistics Seminar on Language Awareness*. Longman, London.

Mitchell, R. and Hooper, J. (forthcoming) 'Teachers' views of language knowledge' in *Proceedings of the British Association for Applied Linguistics Seminar on Language Awareness*. Longman, London.

Nicholas, H. (forthcoming) 'Language awareness and second language development' in *Proceedings of the British Association for Applied Linguistics Seminar on Language Awareness*. Longman, London.

Rinvolucri, M. (1984) *Grammar Games*. CUP, Cambridge.

Rutherford, W. E. (1987) *Second Language Grammar: Learning and Teaching*. Longman, London.

Scholfield, P. J. (forthcoming) 'Language awareness and the computer' in *Proceedings of the British Association for Applied Linguistics Seminar on Language Awareness*. Longman, London.

Sharwood Smith, M. (forthcoming) 'Consciousness and the second language learner' in *Proceedings of the British Association for Applied Linguistics Seminar on Language Awareness*. Longman, London.

Sylvester, L. (forthcoming) 'Language awareness on area studies degrees' in *Proceedings of the British Association for Applied Linguistics Seminar on Language Awareness*. Longman, London.

Tinkel, T. (forthcoming) 'Language awareness and the teaching of English Language in the upper secondary school' in *Proceedings of the British Association for Applied Linguistics Seminar on Language Awareness*. Longman, London.

Wright, T. (forthcoming) 'Language awareness in teacher education programmes for non-native speakers' in *Proceedings of the British Association for Applied Linguistics Seminar on Language Awareness*. Longman, London.

Part III
The Wider Bullock Way:
Cox and Beyond

11 Comment on Cox: The Linguistic Concepts of Register and Genre

Alison B. Littlefair

Writing Purposes and Style

The first Cox Report, following the lead of the Kingman Report, is very much concerned with children's awareness of the different purposes of language and its consequent varieties. However, writing which is produced in response to a particular purpose is often described in the Cox Report as having a particular style. 'Style' is perhaps a misleading word in this context, for style is more specifically the writer's individual interpretation of a register of language. The concept of register is hardly mentioned in either report and yet it influences much of the thinking and therefore many of the recommendations.

Register

'Register' is an abstract term which indicates a language variety which is spoken or written in response to a purpose. Register is expressed through patterning which results from the three aspects of the context of situation in which a communication takes place. These aspects have been described by Halliday (1975) as the field, the mode and the tenor. The *field* relates to the content area which is being written or spoken about, the *mode* indicates the method of communication and the *tenor* indicates the communicator's perception of the relationship between the writer/reader and the speaker/listener. The field, mode and tenor of the situation are inter-active and are expressed through language. It is each of these aspects which constrains the choice of language open to a communicator. Thus the author of a science book for young junior pupils should be constrained in terms of vocabulary, use of cohesive ties, conjunctions, voice, mood and tense, to mention some of the linguistic factors involved. The author of a science textbook for older secondary school pupils will conform to different constraints in the linguistic patterns he or she uses.

Genre

The Cox Report uses 'genre' (5.42) particularly, if not solely, in relation to literary texts. However, this ignores the considerable discussion by some systematic functional linguists that genre is itself an abstract concept. Martin (1984) states: 'For us, genre is a staged, goal oriented, purposeful activity in which speakers engage as members of our culture' (p. 28).

This notion is extremely relevant to the way in which both the first Cox Report and the Kingman Report describe language. We teach children the ways in which our society creates meaning. Every society has evolved particular systems of meaning or genres within its individual context. Some cultures transmit such systems through purely oral activities. Others, such as our own, have evolved both written and oral activities. It follows that different written genres are ways of meaning that are recognised by other members of this culture.

A speaker or writer has a certain purpose which is synonymous with a genre of writing or speaking. It is the purpose of writing or of speaking which indicates the form or linguistic shape which the communication will take. The different forms of genres give structure to communications and the register patterning expresses meaning through the medium of language. It is the way in which register patterning works within different genres which is so important for readers of the Cox Report for the recommendations of the Report can be related quite coherently to this linguistic framework.

Describing how Meaning is Conveyed

The Report indicates (3.15) that meanings are conveyed in different ways. We live in a particular culture which has evolved and continues to evolve certain ways of expressing meaning. The Cox Report notes the importance of children understanding that 'messages are conveyed in a variety of forms and contexts' (3.16). Thus there is insistence that children should be aware of and capable of producing different varieties of spoken and written language. It would be simpler to draw together this web of teaching language varieties, if the structure of genre and register were to be described.

Discussing Forms of Expression or Genre

There are some ways of expressing written and spoken communication which are more prestigious in our culture than others. The Cox Report, by its insistence on the importance of children developing different kinds of writing, is really stating that there are forms of expression, or genres, which are significant in our culture. If children do not learn these forms or genres, they are disadvantaged as they continue their education and as they enter the adult world. The Cox Report notes the necessity of finding 'a way of discussing with children the context in which Standard English is obligatory, or appropriate for social reasons' (4.20). Again, a knowledge of the way in which genre and register work would seem to be essential. In this way, teachers could discuss with children what subject is being written about or spoken about, what the implication of the audience might be, and the method and the form of the communication. Having established these points, a discussion about the kind of language which has been used in a book or by the child becomes a more practical suggestion. Text is then related to context in a meaningful way. Further, this kind of discussion would be quite possible in the primary school as well as in the secondary school. In fact, it lends itself to 'language across the curriculum discussion'.

Relating Text and Context

It has already been noted that the linguistic patterns which are used within a genre are constrained by the situation in which a communication is written or spoken. The Cox Report notes the relationship between 'language, situation and purpose' (5.19). A model of genre and register patterning displays the relationship between these concepts in a way which can be more easily translated into a teaching and learning situation.

Many of the suggested elements in a language curriculum (5.23) are related to this pattern, as are the proposed 'stages of reduction' (5.28) in language discussion. The differences in 'style and form' of 'transactional uses of print' and 'various genres of imaginative writing' (9.6) are part of register patterning. In addition, the comprehensive terms for grammatical structure (5.30), for language forms and functions (5.33), for speech act (5.34), and for terms indicating nuance of meaning (5.36) can all be related to the pattern of genre and register in a manner which can only help understanding.

Children's Use of Linguistic Terminology

Some researchers and teachers in Australia (Martin and Rothery, 1986) have introduced young primary school pupils to linguistic terminology in discussions about the structure of different genres. Not only did they not find this to be a problem but it proved to be an effective help to understanding. It is important to note that the terminology used in this Australian experience was not particularly directed to the study of literature but rather to the understanding of how different genres were structured. Thus children began to talk about the orientation, complication and resolution of a narrative and the thesis, argument, and conclusion of an exposition as they discussed their written work. In this way, children were able to talk about the language as well as the content of their writing or of books they were reading.

Attainment Targets in Reading

Any consideration of the linguistic patterning of genre and register will lead to questioning the necessity of the two reading attainment targets described in the Cox Report. If Attainment Target 1 (9.11) was 'the development of the ability to read, understand and respond to all types of writing', and Attainment Target 11 (9.12) was 'the development of reading and information-retrieval strategies for the purposes of study', then there was inference that these skills were seen as separate from other reading development. There has been later amalgamation of the two targets in the National Curriculum Council Consultation Report (1989).

It may well still follow that information retrieval skills will be taught out of context. Even if reading for study purposes is introduced through project work, there is no warning in the Report that information books may provide a reading experience which is full of hazard. The use of these books is part of reading and writing development, an intrinsic part of which is the use of information-retrieval skills. It should be recognised that some information books are specifically simplified for younger children in language which is not really coherent. It should also be recognised that the teacher should be aware of the possible unfamiliar register patterning of some books which cannot easily be translated 'into your own words'.

Reading Narrative and Expository Texts

There was considerable inference in the Cox Report that narrative would be used in order to attain Target 1 and expository texts to attain Target 11. The ability to read narrative is not the automatic key to an ability to read other genres. If children are to develop flexible reading skills, they must have experience of reading and listening to different genres from their earliest days in school. Indeed, it may be that as the Cox Report suggests (4.2), teachers may have to teach some genres specifically.

Independence as a Reader

One way of explaining 'independence as a reader' (9.7) would be to ask whether a child understands the way in which authors achieve meaning – not an understanding easily achieved. The Cox Report urges teachers to help children to understand 'how meaning is expressed and how effects are achieved in writing' (9.9). This is a daunting task but one which is more manageable if teachers are more explicitly aware of the way in which genres and register are patterned.

Understanding of the way in which written language represents meaning is more likely to be achieved when children's experience of reading and writing is inter-active. Again the different kinds of writing noted in 10.30 can be described as different genres and related to genres which the children read. Most children narrate events when they first write. It might also be that not all children wish to develop as story writers but perhaps as reporters. The two purposes represent different forms or genres of writing, both of which can be described to children and encouraged from an early age. The key to the assessment of the writing of these two genres may well be the child's awareness of developing linguistic structure as well as in the content.

Writing Targets

Attainment Target 1 for Writing is really describing the different aspects of register patterning and the development of constructing different genres as are the points noted in 10.33. If children are to discuss 'the organisation of their own writing' (10.38) they must be taught the way in which different written genres are formed. Indeed, the weighting indicated (10.41) necessitates such teaching if 70 per cent of the assessment is to reflect 'a growing ability to construct and convey meaning in written language.'

An Inter-active Language Framework

The Cox Report is organised so that the different aspects of language use are systematically discussed. Clearly, these aspects are inter-active. The linguistic concepts involved are often concerned with the register patterning and with different genres. An understanding of these factors provides a common language framework to which many of the observations, suggestions and attainment targets can be referred.

References

Halliday, M. A. K. (1975) *Learning How to Mean*. Arnold, London.

Martin, J. (1984) *Language, Register and Genre in Language Studies. Children Writing: Reader*. ECT 418. Victoria, Deakin University.

Martin, J. and Rothery, J. (eds) (1986) *Writing Project*. Working Papers in Linguistics, 4. Sydney University.

12 A Future for Phonics 44

Joyce M. Morris

Over the years my publications, research projects, teaching and other professional activities at home and abroad have covered almost every aspect and level of developing literacy in primary English. A number of influential writers in the same field appear to be either unaware of this fact or they choose to ignore it. For, whenever they mention me, they tend nowadays to draw attention solely to my concern that phonics should be regarded as an essential ingredient of educational provision for literacy.

This could be all to the good if, as is often the case, they did not omit relevant information. For instance, they generally fail to restate my reasons for a concern about phonics which is shared by respected colleagues around the world, and is indisputably valid in terms of the nature of English orthography and the findings of reputable classroom research. They usually also neglect to point out how the system I devised and called 'Phonics 44' (see Appendix, p. 119) differs in educationally significant ways from other kinds of phonics.

Regrettably this type of biased reporting by omission does not stop at being unfair and unhelpful. Amongst other things, it has led to the blanket condemnation of phonics by a vociferous minority of so-called progressive educationists. In turn, to my knowledge, this has caused many class teachers to fear that, if they declare their support for phonic instruction, they will be labelled 'reactionary' and thereby ruin their chances of promotion. Indeed, so great is this fear that, on certain memorable occasions, it has been confided to me literally in whispers by in-service course members. This is because they have wanted me to know that they agree with me about the place and value of phonics, but dare not say so publicly.

Recently, I have begun to believe that the introduction of the National English Curriculum will do a great deal to settle the debate about phonics which has brought such fear in its wake. I have also reason to believe that it will help to ensure a future for Phonics 44. What is more, I am not alone in this belief, and that is basically why I have been invited to make this contribution.

Salient Features of Phonics 44

The rationale for these beliefs naturally lies in a consideration of both the National Curriculum proposals for Primary English and the salient features of Phonics 44.

Phonics 44 is a graphic processing system devised to meet needs revealed by school-based research and the detailed analysis of classroom materials for initial literacy. As details of its origins are given elsewhere (Morris, 1984), it is sufficient to note in this context that the system's unique linguistic structure was derived from research which, amongst other things, involved extensive vocabulary analyses. In short, a very important feature of Phonics 44 is that it is thoroughly research-based and, as will be seen, is 'linguistics-informed'.

The Sound–Symbol Base

What then is the linguistic structure of Phonics 44? First of all, its name and sound–symbol base reflect the relationships found in number and frequency between the 44 phonemes (speech sounds) of the 'standard' accent of British English known as Received Pronunciation (or RP for short) and the graphemes (letters singly and/or in combination) which represent them in traditional orthography.

From the main vocabulary analyses, these relationships or 'correspondences' total 396 but, according to the criteria established, less than 10 per cent are classed as 'divergencies' or 'irregular' spellings. Moreover, this small percentage includes comparatively few words like the word 'one' which are 'hopelessly' irregular, whilst most of the rest fall into divergent groups such as the group of words containing vowel digraphs *ea* and *ow*, corresponding respectively to the vowel sounds in 'bread' and 'snow' rather than to those in 'seal' and 'clown'. In short, one of the salient features of Phonics 44 is that it is a research-based system which dispels that age-old myth that English spelling is hopelessly chaotic and, therefore, reading and/or spelling problems are inevitable for a sizable proportion of the population in English-speaking countries. In doing so, it also supports the use of phonics in general for initial literacy and, at the same time, undermines the rationale usually given for exclusive look–say approaches whether by whole word, phrase, sentence, paragraph or whole story text as, for example, in 'shared reading'.

The Didactic Sequence at Alphabet Level

Children usually begin to learn about sound–symbol correspondence in an informal manner using alphabet books in which each letter in initial word position is presented in sequence. However, delightful and deservedly popular as most of these books are, they tend to be 'misleading' for beginners in so far as the initial letters of the illustrated words represent several speech sounds as in 'Enormous elephants eagerly eating Easter eggs'. In other words, they are generally a better introduction to dictionaries than to 'code-cracking', and their main function for the very young is to give pleasurable opportunities for language development.

Be that as it may, research at a more formal alphabet level indicates that the didactic sequence for Phonics 44 should be based on a division of the letters (except x) into three groups, with the repetition of some letters for specific and mainly contrastive purposes. Here it should be noted that, although Phonics 44 provides the basic linguistic structure for an economical, didactic 'programme' as in *Language in Action* (Morris, 1974–83), the approach throughout is mainly one of differentiation rather than single sequence. For example, within the three groups of letters shown below, the suggested order of introduction for each letter–sound correspondence in initial word position is not a matter of single sequence. Letters are presented together to highlight contrastive features with regard to capital and lower-case forms, associated letters like Ss/Zz and letters which, perceptually, are particularly confusing as in Group 2. (At subsequent levels of *Language in Action*, the differentiation approach of Phonics 44 is highlighted by such book titles as *King Dan the Dane*, and, in the story texts, by the close proximity of words of similar sound and shape as in 'That *clock's* a *crock*'.)

Group 1.   Tt; Yy; Hh; Ww; Rr; Gg/Jj; Ss/Zz; Cc/Kk/Ss.
Group 2.   BD/bd; PQ/pq; MN/mn; VW/vw; EF/ef; IL/il; UN/un.
Group 3.   Aa; Ee; Ii; Oo; Uu.

Learning to read and spell English words involves acquiring the knowledge that the eleven different letters in Group 1 play several different and/or complementary roles in traditional orthography including, notably, their contribution to letter clusters such as the digraphs *sh*, *ch* and *th*. However, it is important that children first appreciate how single letters correspond to phonemes (speech sounds) at the beginning of words before proceeding to learn the function of letter clusters in initial, medial and final word position. It should also be noted that because of the duplicate role of letter *c*, the eleven consonant letters in Group 1 correspond to only ten different consonant sounds in initial word position, whereas Groups 2 and 3 together introduce a further fourteen letters corresponding to thirteen different sounds, thereby covering the alphabet in terms of individual sound–symbol correspondence and leaving the six remaining consonant sounds (numbers 19 to 24 inclusive as indicated in Table 12.1) to be highlighted in the spelling pattern progression which is another educationally significant feature of Phonics 44.

Table 12.1

Consonant sound		Key word
19	as in	ri*ng*
20	as in	*sh*op
21	as in	*ch*imp
22	as in	*th*en
23	as in	*th*umb
24	as in	televi*s*ion

The Vowel-Centred, Vertically organised, Spelling Pattern Progression

Phonics 44 is a graphic processing system which is vowel-centred because the vowel representations are a main source of difficulty for beginners learning to read and to spell English words. The vowel phoneme–grapheme sequence is based on frequency of use in words, and as indicated by the numbers given to the vowel sounds. Thus the twentieth and last vowel in the system, as in the word 'gourd', is the least frequent sound in spoken English and, naturally, words in which it is represented are also relatively infrequent in print.

Contrary to popular belief, English orthography is highly patterned. Consequently, Phonics 44 is also a vertically organised system of spelling pattern progression which begins with the division of monosyllables into major sets as follows:

Set A (vowels 1 to 5) Words in which the vowel letter corresponds to a so-called short vowel sound; e.g. **cat, hen, pig, dog, sun**.

Set B (vowels 7 to 10) Words in which marker, modifying or magic *e* signals that the preceding vowel letter corresponds to a so-called long vowel sound; e.g. **ape, eve, ice, ode**.

Set BB (vowels 7 to 10) Words in which vowel digraphs correspond to the same so-called long vowel sounds; e.g. **rain, play; eel, seat; pie, high; oak, toe**.

Set C (vowels 11 to 20) Words in which the rest of the vowel phonemes (10) are represented in different ways; e.g. **hoop, blue, lute; hook; ball, walk, saw, cause, corn, more; star; bird, hermit, purple; mouth, clown; coil, boy; square, chair; eat, deer, here; gourd, poor, cure**.

Within each of the above spelling patterns, the vertical processing system develops monosyllabic words with consonant clusters of various kinds including letter combinations for the six remaining consonant sounds from the alphabet level (numbers 19 to 24 inclusive). For example, the sequence in Set A is as follows.

1 double letters or their equivalents; e.g. pu*ff*, ba*ck*;
2 consonant clusters which occur both at the beginning and at the end of words; e.g. *sk*ip, ri*sk*; *sp*ot, li*sp*; *st*op; lo*st*;
3 other consonant clusters of two or three letters which occur at the beginning or at the end of words; e.g. *cl*ub, *cr*ust, *scr*ap, *str*ap, ste*ps*, sta*nds*, bli*nks*;
4 consonant digraphs which occur both at the beginning and at the end of words; e.g. *sh*ip, fi*sh*; *ch*op, mu*ch*; *th*en, wi*th*; *th*in, mo*th*.

Next, within each set of the major sets of spelling patterns, disyllabic words are introduced; for instance, present tense forms of verbs such as **skipping** (Set A), **making** (Set B), **painting** (Set BB) and **shouting** (Set C). Also introduced are disyllabic words containing the 'schwa' or weak stress vowel (number 6) in, for example, comparative adjectives such as **redder** (Set A), **nicer** (Set B), **fainter** (Set BB) and **louder** (Set C). Here it should be remembered that, in many verbal contexts, the 'schwa' vowel is also represented in monosyllables as in the very frequent word **the**.

The system also allows for the sequential introduction of words containing the so-called silent letters, in addition to 'silent' marker **e** words. Thus words such as **knit** and **thumb** (Set A) are followed by **knave** (Set B).

Phonics 44 and Primary English in the National Curriculum

Turning now to a consideration of English in the National Curriculum (DES, 1989a), the following list of some of the targets for initial literacy (Key Stage 1) gives some idea of the potential use of Phonics 44 to help achieve those targets.

Spelling

Starting with spelling, as this actually follows from the spelling pattern progression of Phonics 44 summarised above, the targets which most closely relate to the system (with the examples given) are as follows.

Level 1 Pupils
should be able to*   write some letter shapes in response to speech sounds and letter names, e.g. initial letter of own surname.

Level 2 Pupils
should be able to*   spell correctly, in the course of their own writing, simple monosyllabic words they use regularly which observe common patterns, e.g. **see, car, man, sun, hot, cold, thank**.

*   recognise that spelling has patterns, and begin to apply their knowledge of those patterns in their attempt to spell a wider range of words, e.g. **coat, goat, feet, street**.

Level 3 Pupils
should be able to* spell correctly, in the course of their own writing, simple polysyllabic words they use regularly which observe common patterns, e.g. **teacher**.

* recognise and use correctly regular patterns for vowel sounds (no examples given) and common letter strings, e.g. **-ing, -ion, -ous**.

* show a growing awareness of word families and their relationships, e.g. **grow, growth, growing, grown**.

Reading

The attainment targets for reading at Level 1 are mainly concerned with motivation and an understanding of the meaningful purposes of print and reading. In other words, they have little to do with the 'mechanics' of reading except that pupils should 'begin to recognise individual words or letters in familiar contexts'.

At Level 2 children are expected to have made considerable headway with learning to read. For example, they should be able to 'read a range of material with some independence, fluency, accuracy and understanding' and 'demonstrate knowledge of the alphabet in using word books and simple dictionaries'. They should also be able to 'use picture and context cues, words recognised on sight and phonic cues in reading'.

The document *English in the National Curriculum* (DES, 1989a) contains only this one reference to phonic cues for Key Stage 1 (for children up to the age of seven). However, in the document *English for ages 5 to 16* (DES, 1989b), paragraph 16.9 repeats the need for children to have phonic knowledge, the actual words being, 'able to predict meaning on the basis of phonic, idiomatic and grammatical regularities and of what makes sense in context'. That same paragraph also supports a 'balanced' view of teaching reading which I, for one, have always advocated as a result of my ten years' experience in the classroom, subsequent research in Kent (Morris, 1966) and elsewhere. It does so by respecting the following statement from the Bullock Report (DES, 1975): 'There is no one method, medium, approach, device or philosophy that holds the key to the process of learning to read . . . Simple endorsements of one or another nostrum are of no service to the teaching of reading.'

Some Advantages of Phonics 44

Bearing all this in mind, it is not surprising that no specific suggestions are given in either document as to how children are to be helped to acquire essential phonic knowledge. There are a few clues, but the nearest one gets to ideas for detailed provision to develop decoding and encoding skills at Key Stage 1 are to be found in both documents in the following statements.

Activities should ensure that pupils talk about the ways in which language is written down, in shared reading or writing sessions or in discussion with the teacher, identify words, phrases, patterns of letters and other features of written language which they recognise, and notice how words are constructed and spelled.

As they become familar with the conventions of writing, pupils should be introduced to the most common spelling patterns of consonant and vowel sounds. Pupils should be taught how to spell words which occur frequently in their writing, or which are important to them, and those which exemplify regular spelling patterns.

In view of the continuing debate about 'structure' in initial literacy provision, it is also important to note that in *English for ages 5 to 16*, paragraphs 3.10 and 3.13 respectively draw attention to the fact that, with regard to reading and writing in the primary school, it is essential that children have 'structured and sensitive teaching'. Moreover, although its rationale is still rejected by some, this teaching, as discussed in Chapter 5, should include explicit knowledge about language, with linguistic terms introduced in context and not through drills. Examples of classroom practice are included to show how, for instance, top infants can usefully learn 'vowels' as a cue to articulate knowledge about sound–symbol correspondence.

It is pointed out in paragraph 6.3 that 'substantial programmes of teacher training are required if teachers are themselves to know enough to enable them to design with confidence programmes of study about language'. Such training is now under way, but it will take several years before all teachers of primary English in the National Curriculum have received sufficient to ensure that children achieve the targets for reading and spelling on which this paper is focused.

In the circumstances, it is suggested that teachers and teacher-trainers who have not yet used Phonics 44 might study the system to see what contribution it could make to the successful execution of their respective tasks. As will be seen, it has many advantages and some of them are particularly important. In the first place, Phonics 44 supports the contention of a number of linguists that 'English spelling is a reasonably reliable system based on both sound-to-spelling correspondence and on morphological principles'. Second, it works on the principle of economy in teaching and learning and therefore saves time for both teacher and learner. Third, as incorporated in *Language in Action* (Morris, 1974–83), the system encourages more rapid progress towards independence in reading and spelling. (Look–say basal schemes tend to encourage the development of 'primer parrots', not independent readers able relatively soon to move away from schemes to the individual reading books of children's literature.) Fourth, it also acts in the classroom as an on-the-spot diagnostic instrument in that the learner's true progress is indicated by the ability to read and spell words at the various processing stages.

Probably most important of all, Phonics 44 is based on the systematic study of the English language in spoken and written form and, as such, is a linguistics-informed system. This means that teachers using it gain in professionalism and, hence, are better equipped to evaluate critically the phonic resources available and, in general, to help children with the fundamental task of 'internalising a model of the orthography'.

Future Prospects

Thus, with its unique, research-based linguistic structure, Phonics 44 would seem to have a bright future. This is partly because the National Curriculum for Primary English has some targets for reading, spelling and explicit knowledge about language which the system has been devised to help teachers and pupils achieve.

Already from the private as well as the state sector, there is a growing demand for more publications incorporating Phonics 44, and the first of these, a teaching resource called The Morris-Montessori Word List, will shortly be published by the London Montessori Centre. All this augurs well for a future in which every teacher of initial literacy in English will teach according to the specificity of the language, and phonic resources will be free from the linguistic 'folklore' which mars much of what is available at present. At least, with the introduction of the National English Curriculum, we can be reasonably hopeful that 1990, which has been declared 'International Literacy Year', will mark the beginning of a period in British history when functional illiteracy ceases to be the national problem that has long seemed to be insoluble in all English-speaking countries.

References

Department of Education and Science (1975) *A Language for Life* (The Bullock Report). HMSO, London.

Department of Education and Science (1989a) *English in the National Curriculum*. HMSO, London.

Department of Education and Science (1989b) *English for ages 5 to 16*. HMSO, London.

Morris, J. M. (1966) *Standards and Progress in Reading*. The National Foundation for Educational Research in England and Wales, Slough, Bucks.

Morris, J. M. (1974–83) *Language in Action*. Macmillan Education, London and Basingstoke.

Morris, J. M. (1984) 'Phonics 44 for initial literacy in English', *Reading*, 18, 13–24.

Appendix

26 Alphabet letters	44 Speech sounds*	

21 Consonant letters	24 Consonant sounds	+	20 Vowel sounds

1 b	1 /b/ as in bed	1 /æ/ as in apple, cat
2 c	2 /k/ as in cat,	2 /e/ as in egg, hen
3 d	kid, quilt	3 /ɪ/ as in ink, pig
4 f	3 /d/ as in dog	4 /ɒ/ as in orange, dog
5 g	4 /f/ as in fan	5 /ʌ/ as in umbrella, sun
6 h	5 /g/ as in gum	6 /ə/ as in another
7 j	6 /h/ as in hen	7 /eɪ/ as in ape, rain, play
8 k	7 /dʒ/ as in jam	8 /i:/ as in eve, eel, seat
9 l	8 /l/ as in log	9 /aɪ/ as in ice, pie, high
10 m	9 /m/ as in mop	10 /əʊ/ as in ode, oak, toe
11 n	10 /n/ as in net	11 /u:/ as in hoop, blue, lute
12 p	11 /p/ as in pup	12 /ʊ/ as in hook
13 q	12 /r/ as in rod	13 /ɔ:/ as in ball, walk, saw
14 r	13 /s/ as in sun	cause, corn, more
15 s	14 /t/ as in tub	14 /a:/ as in star
16 t	15 /v/ as in van	15 /ɜ:/ as in bird, hermit,
17 v	16 /w/ as in wig	purple
18 w	17 /j/ as in yak	16 /aʊ/ as in mouth, clown
19 x	18 /z/ as in zip	17 /ɔɪ/ as in coil, boy
20 y	19 /ŋ/ as in ring	18 /eə/ as in square, chair
21 z	20 /ʃ/ as in ship	19 /ɪə/ as in ear, deer, here
	21 /tʃ/ as in chimp	20 /ʊə/ as in gourd, poor, cure
	22 /ð/ as in then	
5 Vowel letters	23 /θ/ as in thumb	
	24 /ʒ/ as in television	
22 a		
23 e		
24 i		
25 o		
26 u		

* Phonetic symbols between slant lines provide the accurate identification of the 44 speech sounds basic to Phonics 44.

13 Literature Working for Literacy

Christopher Winch and Kay Goodall

Literature occupies a central role in the preoccupations of both the Kingman and the Cox committees. The literature that children read and the way that the literature is introduced to them have the potential to engender a deep and lasting enjoyment of reading. According to both reports, the mutually supportive nature of the elements of reading, writing, talking and listening need to be used in an interactive way in order to develop understanding, writing skills and a knowledge of the ways in which language works. The issue we explore in this chapter is the nature of this interactive learning and the extent to which the reports make clear how teachers are to facilitate it.

The Kingman Committee was given, as part of its remit, the task of drawing up a model of language that teachers could use in their work with children and the report should be read with that in mind. The Kingman Report places great emphasis on the place of literature in developing pupils' knowledge of language and in developing their abilities as writers. Kingman offers penetrating examples of how literature might be used: the Report provides examples of passages from the Bible through Shakespeare and Dickens to Auden. Some people might consider that such examples are not particularly relevant to the primary classroom, and those teaching young children may be left wondering which features of these and other texts might be used as points for development. The Cox Report gives a list of recommended authors (pp. 28–9), without any detailed examples of just how their books might be used in a profitable way. Since not all of the works of these authors fulfil the criteria which both committees had already established, the provision of such a list without any advice on selection from

within the writers' works is unfortunate. Given the central importance of literature in the learning of younger children and the
sad absence of examples which could be applied to the primary
classroom, there is a danger that teachers will feel unclear as to
how they might make the bridge between the particular writers'
work and their pupils' apparent needs and interest. High demands
will be made of both schools and children without any clear
guidelines as to how these demands might be met. Perhaps this
omission was deliberate, since the success of teaching literature
depends heavily on the ingenuity and professionalism of good
practitioners, and that was presumed to be the norm. Perhaps,
however, there are teachers who would be greatly helped by more
explicit and detailed examples.

The Cox Report sees the study of literature as informing all
aspects of children's English work. Attainment targets for speaking
and listening make it clear that children's literature can be used
most appropriately as part of the corresponding programmes of
study. For example, at Level 3

Pupils should be able to present real or imaginary events in a connected
narrative to a small group of peers, speaking freely and audibly.

and at Level 5

Pupils should be able to discuss and debate constructively, advocating
and justifying a particular point of view.

(p. 36)

Neither of these statements of attainment in themselves requires
the study of stories, poems or drama. However, such a study,
among other things, is particularly suitable for attaining these
targets. It should go without saying that discussion and listening
of this kind can arise in either an incidental or a planned fashion
out of the overall context of study. While Cox sees the processes
involved in writing and the development of a wide range of writing
for different purposes as important aspects of the overall development of writing skills in the primary school, the ability to write
effective narrative (an ability which may not flourish without
encouragement and structured teaching as well as active learning)
remains an important component of the attainment targets. However, the question remains to what extent the writers of the report
have established, for teachers, how, at Level 4, pupils should be

able to 'produce well-structured narratives with an opening, a setting, characters, a series of events and a resolution' (p. 49). Such a target cannot be achieved without taking into account the spoken language and the reading component of the curriculum as well. Even if the report does not develop the discussion about the ways in which speaking, listening, reading and writing are related, the teachers will have to fill that gap, as well as deal with the matter of interpreting and implementing the Report's recommendations. Children will find it difficult to appreciate how and why stories make use of the elements of narrative without being explicitly introduced to these elements and discussing many examples, particularly arising in the context of their own writing.

In order to produce well-structured narrative pupils will need to concentrate on different aspects of the process at different times. They will need to experience many good examples of successful narrative read to them and within their own reading, they will also need to gain some idea of why some stories work so well.

Although the implications of this position are not worked out in any detail in the Report, there is an indication of how children's literature may be used to develop the writing of children themselves.

They should be encouraged to write fiction, verse and autobiography, diaries, plays, book reviews, in response to the literature that they have enjoyed and shared with their classmates. Literature has a number of important roles to play in improving abilities in writing and speaking and listening, as well as developing the child's imagination and aesthetic sense.

(p. 27)

While this statement offers exciting possibilities it must also challenge the teachers to seek out and construct examples of good practice in a variety of situations that will show such work in a meaningful context. This must then be matched with the abilities and experiences of the children and the statements of attainment. Janet and Allan Ahlberg's *The Jolly Postman and Other People's Letters* might be used as a model in order to produce a wide range of written responses in a variety of forms; the combinations produced by children can be exciting and it is the children themselves who determine the purpose, form and audience (Figure 13.1).

Kingman sees literature and language as intertwined and mutually supportive. The Report states: 'Wide reading and as great an

The School house,

Learning Lane

Rhymshire

Dear Mrs. Porgie,

I wonder if you could come to my office
tomorrow to talk about the behaviour of your son Georgie.
The dinner ladies keep complaining becuase he keeps kising girls
and making them cry. He did it yesterday to mary Muffet and
she ran home and caused a fuss. I think everyone knows about
washas happened to her and this was the final straw. Could you
come at ten oclock when asembly is over.

Yours sincerly,

Mrs. Butler.
Headteacher.

Figure 13.1

experience as possible of the best imaginative literature are essential
to the full development of an ear for language and to a full
knowledge of the range of possible patterns of thought and feeling
made accessible by the power of language' (Chapter 2).

Skilful uses of language can be used to highlight the craft of the
writer which in turn enhances the quality of the pupils' experience.
The reading aloud of pieces of literature, from the bedtime story
to the class novel, is often used in this informal way to heighten
awareness and stimulate interest; these insights in turn give the
pupils more control over their own writing. Television, which
forms a large part of pupils' experience outside school, can also be
used to heighten awareness and stimulate interest in literature.
Kingman states the importance of 'understanding that non-verbal

features contribute to oral communication and that degrees of formality and informality matter', the ability to read non-verbal features being an important strategy used by the developing reader. Programmes such as the beautifully animated version of *The Snowman* by Raymond Briggs, Yorkshire Television's 'Book Tower' and broadcasts which specifically are timed and aimed at classroom use, such as Thames Television's 'Seeing and Doing' (see Hunter-Carsch, 1988), can provide the context for stimulating and developing the relevant discussion, developing a forum in which to discuss interpretation and appreciation, as well as providing an enabling framework for the discussion of grammatical and stylistic techniques.

Children's ability to appreciate fully the impact of many stories and literary devices would be severely limited without this dialogue between teacher and children and between children themselves.

The Cox Committee acknowledged that the ability to go beyond literal meaning of a text is crucial to a proper appreciation of literature. There are many examples in books that are intended for very young children that show irony, ambiguity and humour – but what precisely are the strategies that a teacher might introduce in order to develop comprehension of this implied meaning and how might this be facilitated? The material shows, once again, an overall lack of direction and a vagueness in terms of focusing the content.

Whilst recognising that reading is a complex process and re-affirming the Bullock Report (1975) – 'there is no one method, medium, approach, device or philosophy that holds the key to the process of learning to read . . . Simple endorsement of one or another nostrum are of no service to the teaching of reading' – Cox fails to address the issue of how the variety of strategies needed by the learner reader and the variety of materials suggested might be utilized in a structured and constructive way by the teacher for the benefit of the children. Sharing experiences with books and stories is an integral part of developing literacy; active participation is an essential element whether listening, talking, reading or writing. This view is shared by the Cox Committee as they 'urge' parents to 'share books with their children from their earliest days'. The Report then goes on to say that children will have assimilated the pleasurable and purposeful nature of reading from their parents' example and also by engaging themselves to spontaneous 'pretend-writing' activities. It is unrealistic to assume a uniformity in terms of parental experience of literacy as well as expectations of the language experiences that each child brings to school. Parents may differ in the extent to which they are able to facilitate and support their child's growing curiosity about language, experience of literacy and enjoyment of literature. The reality for each child will be different. It will once again be the teacher's role to ascertain what differences each child brings to school and how to devise a programme for their future development.

A knowledge of how stories work and the functions of print are prerequisites for a child when learning to read. There may be children whose English vocabulary when they start school is quite basic, as happens with some children for whom English is a second language, but they may have a wealth of story experiences from the oral story-telling traditions of their home environment. One recent project (Goodall, 1989) with Pakistani children used this already developed sense of story together with the notions of the functions of written language to help develop literacy in their second language. Denial was not made of mother-tongue literacy in promoting the case for second language literacy, but because of the nature of the English education system and the nature of British society a facility and proficiency in English is their entitlement. Keith Topping's recently reported work on paired reading with peer group partners (1988) was used in the project and the Goodall report showed a more positive attitude to reading and improvement in certain skill areas; the children also showed a more positive attitude to themselves as learner readers.

Kingman clearly recognised the need for plentiful in-service provision (a) if teachers are to grasp an adequate model of language themselves and (b) if they are to be able to apply that model to the development of their pupils' own knowledge and understanding of how language works. It would be inspiring if such in-service provision could directly extend teachers' knowledge of children's literature and confidence in developing the children's enjoyment and appreciation as well as their competence in knowing how the subtleties of their language worked to best effect.

While the Bullock proposals could be ignored by schools (and frequently were), the curriculum documents which issue from the Cox Report will have an altogether different status. It is therefore of the greatest importance that it be recognised that literature plays a vital role in the development of literacy. If literature is to be employed successfully to develop and enhance literacy throughout life, the literal meaning of the statements of attainment must be grasped and, more importantly, teachers will need to be able to infer the kinds of activities that can be designed for children to reach the attainment targets. To that end it would be helpful if teachers could be provided with more examples of the kinds of activity that could be based on a work of literature and would potentially develop children's appreciation as well as achievement right across the programme areas of Speaking and Listening, Reading and Writing. Particularly, for teachers who might initially lack confidence in their ability to develop children's reading and writing through imaginative use of literature, provision of detailed examples would be invaluable. What is now needed to implement the National Curriculum in England is development of a range of practices which teachers can explore with children and share with their colleagues and which allow the literature-related targets to be attained in an enjoyable and educationally beneficial way.

References

Department of Education and Science (1975) *A Language for Life.* HMSO, London.

Department of Education and Science (1987) *Report of the Committee of Enquiry into the Teaching of English Language* (The Kingman Report). HMSO, London.

Department of Education and Science (1988) *English from 5 to 11* (The first Cox Report). HMSO, London.

Department of Education and Science (1989) *English from 5 to 16* (The second Cox Report). HMSO, London.

Goodall, K. (1989) *Towards a Model of Entitlement.* M.Ed. thesis, Crewe and Alsager College of Higher Education.

Hunter-Carsch, M. (1988) 'The Kingman Report: Record Keeping; The Teacher Interaction with Child Record' in teachers' notes on the Language Unit in Thames Television 'Seeing and Doing' programme notes.

14 Making More of Poetry

Christine Anderson and
Keith Gardner

Poetry in the classroom is an area of teaching riddled with prejudice and misunderstandings. It is also a source of uneasiness and insecurity.

'If you don't like poetry yourself you can't teach it', summarises a widespread attitude, which is often linked to the equally common belief, 'I was put off poetry at school', and so many teachers avoid poetry as much as they can.

With this in mind is it possible to approach the subject in a positive way? Certainly we can try.

A useful starting point is to stop treating poetry as a subject to be taught or, even worse, as an esoteric mystery requiring the intervention of a specially gifted priest to unravel and explain. It is not a subject, not mystery and certainly not some obtuse hocus-pocus designed to confuse the uninitiated.

Quite simply, poetry is a specialised use of language which, like any other language form, follows certain patterns and conventions – evaluated, initiated, enjoyed and, perhaps, used as a means of communicating thoughts, feelings and ideas in a unique and effective way.

The characteristics of this specialised language are very clear:

1 An economy in the use of words
2 A disciplined arrangement of structures and forms that are designed to achieve dramatic intensity

Disciplined economy in the use of language seems a useful model to consider when teachers are concerned with enabling pupils to master many facets of communication through writing, reading and speaking. So there is a real practical foundation for examining the virtues and the limitations of the ways of poetic language.

In the primary school this examination can be based on the need to give pupils as wide an experience as possible of the different ways in which language can be used. Thus, what begins as an exploration can become a means for extending a repertoire of strategies used in communication and understanding.

A threefold curriculum framework then emerges.

1   The listening to the language that poets compose, with speaking and thinking about it, sharing it
2   Continued listening and discussing, with trying out of this way of writing, and making tentative hypotheses and evaluations
3   A looking at poetry by minds that have begun to appreciate the problems of disciplined articulation

This sounds rather grandiose, but when the application of these principles to specific age groups is considered, the issues become clearer. Even from the early years this study can be achieved through the analysis of poetic language and the production of it, remembering that originally poetry was meant to be heard.

Early Years

In the early years, pre-school one hopes, children respond to hearing nursery rhymes, jingles, counting rhymes and action rhymes. The steady rhythms and repetition of words and phrases are basic and hypnotic and children repeat them and learn them in spite of the fact that their origins may be shrouded in the Great Plague or the misdemeanours of a princeling. At this stage story told in verse, simple narrative poems, and ballads are also appreciated. It need not all be Humpty Dumpty.

Essays at poetry production begin at a very early age if one considers the babblings and experiments with sounds that infants enjoy. The endless repetitions of favourite sounds-of-the-day, to chortlings and steady beating of some unfortunate toy against the floor, could well be the first attempts of an embryo poet! Later, children delight in coining rude rhymes and nicknames, all playing with sounds and words. As physical dexterity grows, traditional bouncing ball and skipping rhymes can become adapted by the children to topical situations, and new ones invented.

Middle Primary

The exploratory experiences of these early years should become slightly more formalised by middle primary. The rhymes and rhythms which hold the poems together and make them easier to remember than prose should be looked at occasionally. The methods by which poems make their impact can be studied informally.

- What happens if we change a word, substitute a synonym?
- Does the rhythm go? Do we want it go? Is the effect lost?
- Why do these two words sound so well together? Do they make us hear another sound, or see another picture?

A growing awareness of the poet's techniques can lead to some very revealing discussions by children about poems considered to be suitable for these middle years.

Ballads and narrative poems with lots of dramatic action condensed into each stanza, along with colourful descriptions of scene, can be acted out, with taped recitation as accompaniment. This continued active participation, and the necessary repetitions for rehearsal, leads to memorisation of phrases and sentences which often surface again in speech and writing.

The experiments with words and sounds and appropriate language to express and communicate ideas can now be made more concrete. Reading and writing are becoming more fluent and the visual and tangible elements of poetry can be explored. Many children would cling to rhythm and rhyme for the security they give, but freed from them, the children can concentrate on other ways of obtaining a desired effect: through choice of language, the juxtaposition of ideas and images, the shape of the poem, visually now, as well as aurally.

Using a tape recorder can be helpful for sharing, enjoying, exploring and developing children's initial responses, say, to a bunch of dandelions. The tape could be replayed and discussed. A more studied response could then be composed by transposing the words and phrases to cards or a word processor, and physically moving them about! The children can try them out in different positions for sound and sense and suitability. The group might think they have the makings of a poem, and read and show it to the class, whereupon another discussion would no doubt ensue. Not every attempt produces a poem, but the language experience is invaluable.

It is an imposition to ask a child to memorise a poem. The wish to commit something to memory should come from within, as a result of enjoyment of the images evoked and the language used. Memorisation should be commended, however, and it will be accomplished, even in small ways, if children are involved in happy experiences of worthwhile poems. They will spontaneously remember language sequences, verses, even whole poems. Poems and verses on the wall, written large, can be as much part of a wall's decoration as pictures. Some children will remember these vividly.

Upper Primary

All that has been said about middle primary also pertains to upper primary. However, group dramatisation and presentation will become more sophisticated as deeper understanding of poetic language develops, and (choral) speaking and (solo) recitation and reading will become more polished. Fewer physically active poems, more emotive and reflective ones will be investigated, and the different types of verse will have their idiosyncrasies remarked upon and discussed.

If this poetry curriculum has been followed through school, by the upper primary the children should have experienced a rich variety of poems of all kinds, and they should be able to express some feelings and opinions about them. They should know quite a few 'pieces' from memory and some may even have begun their own anthologies.

The varying powers of poetic language should be a possible topic of discussion and some criticial decisions could be reached.

- What kind of poems should we tape for the old ladies in the Old Folks Home?
- What verses should we tape for the old man who has become blind? He's an artist. He used to paint pictures . . .
- What kind of poems should we put on a video for the children's convalescent home?

When it comes to producing poetry in upper primary, with many models to choose from, some children will produce adequate parodies. But the study of the poetic language and devices employed should continue and by now can become more explicit.

- What is the rhyming scheme of this ballad?
- How does this limerick hang together?
- What effect does the change in the traditional scansion of this verse have on us?

There is no reason why the pupils should not be offered the chance of learning a more official vocabulary.

To assist in this discussion of techniques why should deletions not be used? A group exercise in completing a verse of poetry with carefully chosen gaps to fill in could be very rewarding, and need not vandalise the whole poem.

- Why is a two-syllabled word needed here?
- This word certainly rhymes correctly but does it make sense?
- Does this word conjure up an exciting image, or sound?

Or convert the following limerick into a traditional one, correctly rhymed and scanned, by altering the underlined words:

There was an old man from Dunoon,
Who always ate soup with a fork
He said – Since I eat
Neither fish, fowl nor flesh,
I would finish my dinner too quickly. (Anon.)

As a relief from language study, the lives of some famous poets could give colour to the scene – for example, the heroic charisma of Byron, the romance of the Brownings . . . Furthermore, the place and importance of poetry in some people's lives is often surprising and discussing this can help dispel the myth that poetry is only for children and people in love. It is more than the sentimental verses in greeting cards; it can be a source of calm and comfort to politicians and soldiers, inspiration to the down-trodden and the rallying cry of armies. Such revelations are frequently surprising.

We have dealt with poetry here as a study of specialised language. As such its importance lies in the many different effects it can have on the individual listeners or readers as well as writers. During poetry study in school many pupils will experience these effects having looked at how these forces are produced, they will be able to evaluate them.

In these days of language manipulation by the media, the study of poetic techniques can give us some insight and appreciation of the subtleties of meaning that language can produce. It is not impossible to initiate primary school children, through poetry, into this liberating power.

The appended list of some references to poetry in the National Curriculum proposals in the second Cox Report may be of interest to readers who are making the connection between this chapter, their own views, and the classroom.

One of the best ways of developing and sharing ideas for teaching poetry is to have a poetry workshop. Such workshops provide opportunities for writers, teachers (and teachers who are also writers), speakers and readers to share their creative work, responses and suggestions. Successful workshops have taken place at UKRA regional day conferences (such as the one held in Leicester in 1987) and national conferences (such as those held in Cramond, Edinburgh in 1987, Leicester in 1988 and Ormskirk in 1989); there is also one on the programme for the July 1990 conference at Nottingham University.

Appendix

Explicit References to Poetry in English for ages 5 to 16

15.24   Attainment Target 1: Speaking and Listening

Level 1. ii   Listen attentively and respond to stories and poems.

Level 2. iii   Listen attentively to stories and poems, and talk about them.

Level 4. iv   Participate in a presentation, e.g. of the outcome of a group activity, a poem, a story or a scene.

Level 5. v   Plan and participate in a presentation, e.g. of the outcome of a group activity, a poem, story, dramatic scene or play.

15.28   Programme of Study for Speaking and Listening: Detailed provisions for Key Stage 1

- telling stories and reciting poems which have been learnt by heart
- listening and responding to the presentation or performance of an increasing range of fiction, poetry and plays

15.33 Detailed provisions for Key Stage 2 (ages 7 to 11) Pupils working towards Level 4 . . . The range of activities should be widely varied including the preparation of presentation . . . undertaking assignments where specific outcomes are required, talking about stories and poems and taking part in shared writing activities . . . encouraged to contribute individually in class discussion and where practicable with wider audiences . . .

15.38 (ii) Pupils working towards Level 7 . . . Teaching should cover discussion about the situations in which and purposes for which people might choose to use non-standard varieties rather than Standard English, e.g. in speech with friends, in a local team or group, in television advertising, folk songs, poetry, dialogue in novels or plays.

16.6 There should be opportunities for individual and group reading activities, which might lead to 'performance readings' of text of different genres, especially drama and poetry . . .

16.10 . . . Well chosen picture books, poetry collections, folk tales, stories, novels, reference books and non-fiction should be available for use in all primary classrooms . . .

16.13 . . . Learning to read involves recognising that writing is made . . . poets were originally called 'makers', crafts-men and women . . .

16.14 . . . we particularly urge that children should be encouraged to write fiction, poetry, plays, diaries, book reviews and so on in response to the literature they have enjoyed and shared and discussed with their teacher and classmates.

15 Finding a Voice through Drama

Ken Byron

This paper addresses four questions:

1 What is Drama in Education? This section introduces a model based on what I believe to be the best in current thinking and practice. The model assumes that drama in education, though often operating in ways that appear dissimilar to adult theatre, is in fact using the same basic 'clay' that all forms of drama employ.

2 What can Drama in Education do? Some of the major ways it can contribute to a genuinely broad and balanced curriculum are examined. This outline assumes that the dichotomy often posited between drama as an art form and as a learning medium is ill-founded. Drama's power as a learning medium resides in its specific nature and dynamic as an art form.

3 What is its relationship to the teaching of English? Here a brief theoretical statement is offered examining how drama can assist the teaching of speaking and listening, reading and writing. Drama's contribution here is seen very much as an aspect of its overall contribution to the curriculum, not simply as an activity for 'English lessons'.

4 What should we make of the Cox Report on drama? The relevant portions of the report are briefly summarised and commented upon.

1 What is Drama in Education?

Drama occurs when a group of people (drama is a social art) agree, for a certain time, to attend to a set of fictional events 'as if' they were occurring 'here and now'. That is the essential contract between actors and audience in the theatre, and between partici-pants in a classroom drama. Whereas in a theatre the 'participant' and 'spectator' roles are allocated separately to actors and audience respectively, in the classroom participants are also the spectators to their own actions in the play they are making, and the best drama practice involves a subtle interplay between the engagement of 'being there' and a more reflective distancing.

Like any art form drama has its own dynamic and 'laws' – that, for example, drama depicts people operating under tension, in the present moment, with past events and future consequences pressing upon them. Participants in classroom drama need to learn to respect the demands and harness the opportunities of the art form. One characteristic that distinguishes drama from other art forms is its semiotic richness. Literature, for example, restricts its signing, as a general rule, to printed symbols with some supplementary use of visual pattern – the layout of words on the page. Drama can exploit verbal as well as written language signs, and other signs such as gesture, movement and stillness, visual configurations and patterns (in three-dimensional space), non-verbal sound, costume, and objects. In drama we 'read' and 'write' using all the sign systems that are available to humankind.

The best classroom drama practice involves a strong interventionist role for the teacher, who often participates in the drama itself, as well as leading discussion sessions which plan and reflect on the work. The teacher's function is partly to assist the class to become progressively more skilled at handling the medium of drama, at 'reading' and 'writing' drama signs, at first encouraging mainly intuitive response and understanding, then working over time towards a more conscious grasp of drama form. Another function of the teacher is, through questioning, through the building in of dilemmas, contradiction and complexity, through fostering the children's struggle to 'make sense' of the experiences explored in the drama, to steadily help them to deepen their understanding of the social world they inhabit and of the values that inform it, and to develop their own personal value system. Drama engages both mind and heart, and brings them into relationship: as Bertolt Brecht wrote, 'One thinks feelings and feels thoughtfully'.

2 What can Drama in Education do?

As the Calouste Gulbenkian Report, *The Arts in Schools*, pointed out, the arts are distinctive ways of knowing and understanding the world and constitute an essential part of any curriculum which seeks to develop in students the full range of human rationality. Drama has an irrefutable contribution to make as a way for children to explore their moral, social, cultural and political world, a way which brings intuition, feeling, logical thought and values into relationship with each other. It is, if you like, one of the 'languages' humankind has forged in its long history of interrogating the world and our existence in it. It is a part of culture children are entitled to have access to.

Drama in education has a number of features which make it a very powerful tool for learning, and allow it to be used extensively across the curriculum. Because we can step into any context we wish, 'as if' we were there, drama allows us to expand exponentially the range of contexts we can explore in the classroom 'at first hand'. Drama moreover provides an overall context within which a wide variety of other curriculum activities can be folded in – a drama-based exploration of the Amazon rain forest could take in a study of aspects of biology, botany and ecology; an exploration of Amazon Indian culture; creative work in music and visual art; an examination of issues of power, land and money – of the relation between rich and poor in Brazil, and between the developed and the developing world; as well as a potentially enormous range of language opportunities – for speaking and listening, reading and writing. The drama context allows these different activities to be linked together in a coherent pattern of understanding in a way that a conventional approach to a classroom 'topic' does not always do.

The driving force of drama is a felt tension (or tensions) – it derives its energy from the efforts of the characters to resolve a disturbance, to restore equilibrium to a situation that is out of balance. I find an interesting parallel with the way learning occurs: the struggle for understanding begins with a disturbance caused by an imbalance or contradiction or blockage in the learner's grasp of the phenomena s/he is faced with. This generates a felt tension, a need to find a resolution of the problem. Perhaps this is why drama in education is such a powerful, *generative* way of working in the classroom – from the simplest situations, large questions arise, long vistas for further explorations open up.

Because students in a classroom drama are both participants and spectators to their own action, they bring an unusually high degree of reflective awareness to their own behaviour, thinking and language.

Since drama is the most concrete and 'life-like' (semiotically rich) of all the art forms it plays to children's strengths as learners because of their 'relatively well-developed capacity for making sense of certain types of human situations involving direct and immediate human interaction'. Yet dramatic action is not simply concrete. It is in fact always an abstraction embodied in concrete action. As Vygotsky (1976) pointed out, it is through dramatic play that the young child is first able to move beyond what is in his/her perceptual field, and to make thought predominate over action. Drama is a powerful vehicle for allowing that gradual movement from 'embedded' to 'disembedded' thinking that Margaret Donaldson (1978) argues is the major demand that schools place on children (p. 36).

Drama as an intensely collaborative art has a major contribution to make in fostering a form of education which Dewey (1938) described as 'a social enterprise in which all have the opportunity to contribute and to which all feel a responsibility' (p. 71). The interventionist model of drama teaching I referred to earlier allows the teacher to influence directly and significantly the way the class functions as a learning community. It also allows for significant and productive shifts in relationships between teachers and learners (as well as between learners and learners), because interactions in role may be radically different to those normal in a conventional classroom situation. And finally it assists children to operate 'ahead of their own development'.

I refer here to Vygotsky's (1978, p. 86ff.) concept of the zone of proximal development – the difference between what children can achieve with appropriate support from and interactions with others, and what they can achieve alone. In Vygotsky's view what children can achieve with support and interaction 'today' is what they will be able to achieve alone 'tomorrow'. The best drama practice is characterised by a powerful combination of support for, and challenge to, students, which I would argue helps them to operate 'a head taller' than themselves.

3 What is its Relation to the Teaching of English?

The kind of uses for drama in the curriculum which I have been describing all assume a central role for language – language used purposively in context. As we engage in, plan, or reflect on our classroom dramas, we talk and listen, read and write both to develop and consolidate our understanding and to communicate it to each other.

A recent Australian research report (Parsons et al., 1984) provides clear evidence of the rich range of language use drama offers. It demonstrates a far wider range of language use in drama sessions than was found generally in primary classrooms, which tended to be dominated by informational language. The drama lessons revealed a much higher use of expressive and interactional language, with a far greater degree of generalisation and abstraction, and much more complex syntactical structures.

Language is shaped by the context, and the roles, relationships and intentions of those present. I have already explained that we can create any ('as if') context for learning that we wish. I now suggest that we can create any combination of 'as if' context, roles, relationships and intentions – in short *any* language demand we wish within a drama, not to mention language work that might follow from the drama. I am referring not only to speaking and listening, but also to reading and writing – even including such processes as redrafting, checking for errors, or producing the best possible presentation of a document: the role of monks copying out the gospels at Lindisfarne is a wonderful incentive to improve handwriting! What drama supplies is the *need* to use or decipher language, spoken or written, and the pressure to 'get it right', because in a drama people's lives may hang on the wording of a speech or a document. The fiction provides a pressure that would be unreasonable (even immoral) for teachers to exert in the 'real' world of the classroom. It is legitimate because the fiction also protects – it is 'only' a drama: there will be no real consequences.

Part of drama's power, then, to extend language resides in its capacity to engage us emotionally, to help us feel that we are 'there' so that we reach intuitively under the imminent pressure of the situation for the words (and actions) that seem right. But accompanying that participant engagement is the spectator dimension – we are aware that this is a fiction, and even as we engage intensely in it, we watch it unfold with a certain detachment. Later we step out of the drama and talk about what 'they' (the people in the drama) did, thought, felt and said and about how we feel the drama worked. There is an oscillation between engagement with the experience and reflection on it, and on how the experience was structured dramatically, and perhaps on how it might be differently structured. This spectator mode brings a strong degree of awareness of how language, among other elements, is being used in the drama.

4 What should we make of the Cox Report on Drama?

First of all, there is a strong sense of *déjà vu* – drama practitioners rush anxiously to the latest weighty official government document on the curriculum, to see if drama gets a mention, and finding it does, they breathe an enormous sigh of relief and start to register their gratitude for being allowed a place (if only small) in the sun. However, the Cox and National Curriculum Council reports seem to me to be full of contradictions in their treatment of drama.

On the one hand, their general statements indicate that drama is 'a good thing' – 'central in developing all major aspects of English in the primary school' (Cox); 'all children should have the opportunity to use role-play and improvised drama as part of their learning' (NCC).

A rather bland 'liberal' endorsement is given to various uses for drama; for example,

- opportunities for children to experience 'different points of view';
- its contribution to 'personal growth, by enabling children to express their emotions', and to growth in personal confidence;
- offering scope for them to function 'collaboratively';
- the chance to 'practise' varieties of language in different situations. (Note *'practise'* not *use*, and note that the power of drama context in the area of reading and writing is ignored; drama's contribution is seen as only in 'speaking and listening'.

Cox rightly emphasises the value of process as against product, and tries to insist on the range of drama's contribution to the curriculum – denying that its inclusion within English is a replacement for specialist study, and arguing for the use of role-play to 'inform' other areas of the curriculum such as science and history. In doing so it unfortunately adopts the old dichotomy of 'creative art form' and 'learning tool'.

On the other hand we have the references to drama in the attainment targets, and in the related examples. There instrumentalism and reductionism rule, OK? Drama is used to see if the child can convey clear messages; can act out stories – a practice the DES survey on drama in schools was querying as long ago as 1967; can 'plan and present, with others, a dramatic scene or play'. There is no trace here of the rich and subtle gains in drama practice accumulated over the last 20 years. It is as if they had never occurred.

I listened at a recent (April 1989) conference to Roger Samways, the one member of the Cox working party who seems to have an informed awareness of the nature and potential of drama in education, arguing that from the starting point of the required reading given to that committee – which appeared largely to originate from the Centre for Policy Studies – they had been able to achieve a considerable movement. Citing the paragraphs on drama and the admirable quotations from David Allen on the basic requirements of teaching and learning, he was able to say in effect, 'Look what we managed to get into the report'.

He had to concede the narrowness of the references to drama in the attainment targets and the associated examples and he acknowledged that there was an acute danger that the general endorsement given to drama would fade from people's minds (and practice) as they dealt with what alone had statutory force – the programme of study and the attainment targets. Pressures like publication of school results and open enrolment will, I am sure, work to reinforce such tendencies. We are under pressure to regard education as a commodity; the curriculum as something to be 'delivered', and the school as a business to be marketed.

The best of current drama in education practice represents a powerful ensemble method of inquiry into the social world. It stands in stark opposition to the strange but dangerous mixture of traditional academicism and new adaptive vocationalism which the current government wishes to see imposed on education. They seek to impose a new language on education, and, as we all know, words carry values. Drama in education seeks to enable students to develop their own 'voice'.

Perhaps in the long run that is the most important kind of 'language development'. Perhaps drama and English, as powerful tools for cultural enquiry, can act in partnership to work for a far broader, fuller and richer educational entitlement than the National

Curriculum could possibly give. Perhaps we can take advantage of the official pronouncements:

• that the National Curriculum has to be set 'in the context of the whole school curriculum';
• that teaching does not have 'to be organised and delivered within prescribed subject boundaries';
• and that 'making sure . . . that good practice is picked up and spread, is essential to ensuring an up-to-date and valuable National Curriculum'.

Perhaps we can work to develop practice that, while taking account of National Curriculum requirements, is not overly constrained by them; practice that begins to reveal the limitations of the National Curriculum, and helps in the long term towards a new and radically improved National Curriculum. I would urge readers not to allow themselves to become depressed by what is being imposed by government, but to use the pressure as a spur to sharpening professional practice, thinking and dialogue. The game is *not* lost. There is everything still to play for.

References

Calouste Gulbenkian Foundation (1982) *The Arts in Schools: Principles, Practice and Provision*. Calouste Gulbenkian Foundation, London.
Dewey, J. (1938) *Experience and Education*. Macmillan, New York.
Donaldson, M. (1978) *Children's Minds*. Fontana, London.
Parsons, B., Schaftner, M., Little, G. and Felton, H. (1984) *Drama, Language and Learning*. National Association for Drama in Education, Paper No. 1, Australia.
Vygotsky, L. S. (1976) 'Play and its Role in the Mental Development of the Child' in Bruner, J. S., Jolly, A. and Sylva, K. (eds) *Play: Its Development and Evolution*. Penguin, London.
Vygotsky, L. S. (1978) *Mind and Society*. Harvard University Press, Cambridge, Mass.

16 Organising for Talk

Margaret Litchfield

Talk and listen, both in groups and in a whole class, in a variety of forms: narrating, explaining, justifying, describing situations and feelings, giving instructions and conveying information, playing a role, putting forward and countering an argument.

Attainment Target 14 at age 11 (DES, 1987)

These planned situations should embrace talk and listening, with both peers and adults and a wide variety of groupings.

(DES, 1988, para. 8.18)

These two recommendations both informed and are reflected in this chapter.

The guidelines provided in Kingman and the first Cox report are so condensed it requires application to the classroom context to explore what their applications really are. It was exciting to do this systematically analysing the actual formal and functional categories of the utterances of a sample of twenty-five children working in a variety of organisational settings in a Leicestershire primary school classroom.

Oracy

Oracy is a fledgling field without a common definition. Broadly speaking three main strands can be identified in the literature:

1   Talk as a medium for learning across the curriculum, holding equal validity with reading and writing
2   Talk as a medium worthy of teachers' attention in its own right as they help children improve their effectiveness as communicators

3 Talk as a medium for assessing children's knowledge. This aspect is endorsed by the suggested assessment procedures included in the three areas of the National Curriculum in its present form.

These three strands should not be perceived as in opposition to each other; rather, they are complementary. One could draw a parallel in that if 'we learn to read by reading' then, arguably, 'we learn to talk by talking' (Smith, 1982). This chapter, however, is more concerned with the first two strands which raise two fundamental questions for the teacher, as Jones (1988) points out:

1 'What kinds of talk should the children be exposed to, trying out and developing in the classroom?'
2 'How can I create opportunities for these kinds of talk to happen?'

The first question raises issues of nomenclature, of finding a satisfactory and preferably simple framework which is practical, easy to apply but informative. The second raises organisational issues.

In an attempt to come to grips with the first question a colleague and I looked at existing frameworks for analysing classroom oral interaction and found what seemed to be various anomalies.

1 Some frameworks operate separate categorisation procedures for children's and teachers' talk with the child in a dependent position as it is the teacher who shapes the dialogue. This, apart from presenting a heavily directive model of the learning process and unrepresentational of reality, also makes discourse analysis impossible.
2 Some frameworks exclude children's questions, not because they consider them unimportant but because they seem to belong more to form than function.
3 Many frameworks include 'imaging' or 'role play'. However, it seems to us that this, along with its opposite 'real life', is part of the context of talk rather than a function, since in both modes one still narrates, reports, describes, etc.
4 Some categorisations combine aspects of form, function and context with what might be termed characteristics of talk – hesitation, repetition, 'thinking pauses'. While we do not deny

the value of the information that observation of the latter provides, they do not seem to fit with purposes for talk.

A growing concern also was the increase in published schemes or courses purporting to develop oracy skills at both primary and secondary levels. We agree with Barnes (1971): 'Spoken language should be developed in a context of living issues, of critical enquiry into how the world is, not of neutralised pseudo-topics invented solely to give a semblance of content to talk for talk's sake. The context for speech is the whole curriculum.'

These, then, became our two aims:

1   To examine the effects that classroom organisation and curriculum tasks have on both pupils' and teachers' language.
2   To tentatively identify a manageable number of easily recognised functions of talk, applicable to both teachers' and pupils' language, which would enable teachers to:
     (a) evaluate the current language life of their classrooms;
     (b) plan specific curriculum tasks in specific organisational groupings to provide the breadth, balance, relevance and differentiation of experiences necessary for optimum language growth.

A Classroom Project

We approached Folville Junior School, Leicester. With the active encouragement of the headteacher and the willing participation of a fourth-year class and their teacher, we videotaped the activities listed below. The criteria for choosing this particular class were that flexible grouping and recognising the central place of talk were accepted practice. The children's names and transcripts of discussions are included in the course of this chapter.

1   *The invitation*   This was a discussion between the teacher and the whole class to formulate a written response to a supposed invitation from Princess Diana to visit Buckingham Palace.
2   *Fund raising A and B*   Two discussions between the teacher and two different groups of four children (mixed sexes), on how they were going to organise various fund-raising activities (a disco, a raffle, stalls) whose proceeds were to be divided between class needs and charity.

3 *Redrafting A and B* A is a discussion between the teacher and a girl on improving the clarity and continuity of a story she had written. B is a similar discussion with a boy, about his story, but is more concerned with choice and variety of vocabulary.

4 *Marie-Celeste* Two boys and two girls argue the fate of the ship from a set of given alternatives provided in their English course book.

5 *Problem solving A and B* Two groups of children (six in one, three in the other, both including boys and girls) try to design a structure which will enable a marble to travel down a slope in a given amount of time.

6 *Cube* A boy and girl have to work out presenting faces from two-dimensional images.

7 *Pond* A boy and girl are engaged in collecting a variety of wild life from the school pond.

As we later observed the videotapes, a possible model for assessing the children's talk began to emerge. Still 'ducking' the challenge presented by having to analyse *'function'* we thought useful information might be gained from separating it from *'form'* and looking at the latter. Since there are only four grammatical forms in English this is a manageable task.

Types of Form, Coding and Examples from the Transcripts

1 *S – Statement* 'I can't think', 'No, not really, no', 'You're not in a hurry', 'We can get broken biscuits for fifty pence for a great big box off my grandad.'

2 *Q – Question* If wished, questions can be further broken down:
   (a) 'Wh' words – 'Where could Adam go?', 'If you're excited, how do you say things?'
   (b) Inversion – 'Can you see the big gap?', 'Did you?'
   (c) Tag endings – 'You're coming, aren't you?', 'That's right, eh?'
   (d) Intonation – 'Cellar?', 'And they believed you?'
      In addition, 'o' can be added for open questions – 'What do you think?' – and 'cl' for closed – 'What time does it start?'

3 *I – Imperative* 'Slow down', 'Cut, cut, cut', 'Turn that once and knock it down.'

4 *E – Exclamation* 'Great!', 'Well done!', 'Ugh!'

Table 16.1 An analysis of form (%)

Title	Participants	t.u.	p.u.	t.q.	p.q.	t.s.	p.s.	t.i.	p.i.	t.e.	p.e.
The invitation	T + class	46	54	24	5	18	48	1	0	2	2
Fund raising A	T + 4 children	32	68	19	7	11	60	1	0	1	1
Fund raising B	T + 4 children	25	75	13	2	16	67	0	0	2	2
Redrafting A	T + 1 child	50	50	35	0	8	49	8	0	0	0
Redrafting B	T + 1 child	50	50	32	4	16	47	1	0	0	0
Marie-Celeste	4 children		100		6		94		0		
Problem solving A	6 children		100		7		55		38		
Problem solving B	3 children		100		22		52		24		
Cube	2 children		100		13		80		5	2	2
Pond	2 children		100		13		67		15	2	5

t.u., teacher; p.u., pupil; t.q., teacher questioning; p.q., pupil questioning; t.s., teacher statement; p.s., pupil statement; t.i., teacher imperative; p.i., pupil imperative; t.e., teacher exclamation, p.e., pupil exclamation

As Table 16.1 shows, there are different patterns – both in terms of taking 'turns' and use of different linguistic forms occasioned by different groups and tasks. One interesting finding is that contrary to an original personal hypothesis that frequency of pupil-generated questioning would rise sharply when the teacher was not present, it did not rise to the percentage of imperatives used in the problem-solving task. The later increase, however, is important if we acknowledge that giving instructions is an important means of controlling one's world.

We then started to apply the function categories outlined by Kingman and reproduced at the beginning of this article. As we worked we decided to extract 'playing a role' since, as stated earlier, this is a context in which all other functions still occur. For ease we collapsed 'putting forward and countering an argument' into 'argument', since, in our examples, where this occurred, pupils were adept at both. However, we felt we had to add the category 'hypothesis' since this was not covered by existing functions.

Function Categories, Coding and Examples from Transcripts

N – Narration   A sustained account of an event or series of events – for example, retelling a story or recounting what happened at home last night. Narration can be spontaneous or elicited.

E – Explanation 'Cause we'll do one that size and then one'll start going . . .', 'To see if they can get some more money.'

J – Justification 'No, I don't think it's A – in a very bad storm it wouldn't – the storm would wave the thing, and it would break some of the sails on it.'

D – Description   of objects, places, people, events, actions and feelings. 'You've got a super story, a super start, a great middle, you've put the ending on it but it doesn't fit', 'I'd jump for joy.'

I – Instruction 'Pass the scissors.'

Inf – Information 'My dad's six foot', 'Well, it's a long way from Leicester to London.'

H – Hypothesis 'They could've found two ships, could've been there', 'If he looked in the Captain's log . . .'

A – Argument 'You said it was easy', 'I thought it was, it's not.'

In addition we wanted to note when pupils and teachers were eliciting information or hypotheses as distinct from providing them, so question forms are coded by a preceding letter 'e'. A complete 'skeleton' model is provided below.

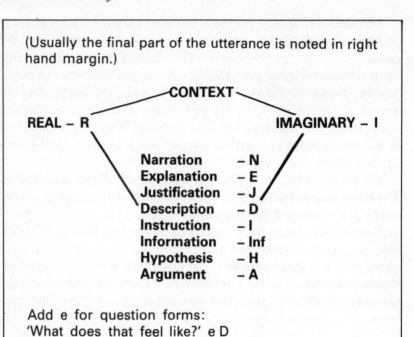

(Usually the final part of the utterance is noted in right hand margin.)

CONTEXT

REAL – R   **IMAGINARY – I**

Narration	– N
Explanation	– E
Justification	– J
Description	– D
Instruction	– I
Information	– Inf
Hypothesis	– H
Argument	– A

Add e for question forms:
'What does that feel like?' e D
'What time does the train leave?' e Inf

In 'marking up' transcripts we decided to categorise only the final parts of lengthy utterances since these are the load bearers of discourse flow. The following is an example of a 'marked up' transcript.

Fund raising

Q *Teacher.* How are you organising your stalls, then?   e Inf

S *Simon.* We're having one stall that had got a lot of girls'   Inf
stuff on and some girls are doing – some girls are organising
that and we're having the boys' toys on the other, er,
table.

Q *Teacher.* Are you sure that girls' toys and boys' toys are   e A
going to fit that easily on to tables? Don't people want to
buy all sorts of different toys?

Q *Robert (to Simon).* I think they could, couldn't they?   A

S *Natasha*. I think that girls like boys' stuff.   A

S *Robert*. Could ask Louise to bring some of those transfers   Inf
in 'cos she's got those things, hasn't she? She's got those
. . .

I *Jennifer*. Put the tables together and then go to there, if   I
they want that, just look through all of them.

I *Simon*. Just put two tables, two tables together and just   I
put all the stuff on, all of them.

Q *Teacher*. That seems a reasonable idea, isn't it?   e Inf

Q *Robert*. And if we use that – they could use that old bin e Inf
or something for the raf – for the lucky dip if . . .
whatever you're doing (*looking at Simon*)?

S *Simon*. I think we're have, yea, I think we'll be having a   Inf
lucky dip.

This example was chosen deliberately to show the firm but sensitive handling by the teacher of Simon's sexist assumptions!

It then becomes possible to chart the transcripts in the following way to examine the different functions of talk that differing situations elicit (Tables 16.2 and 16.3).

The examples shown in Tables 16.2 and 16.3 were chosen for their dissimilar profiles. Table 16.2 displays turns shared equally between the children with the teacher talking more than any individual child. The functional categories most heavily used are 'Information' and 'Argument'. In contrast, Table 16.3 shows weighting to 'Instruction' (also, where was Rajinder, and why did she make no contribution at all?).

This work is at a very early, explorative stage. We make no claims for generalisation; indeed, it is likely that each class and its teacher would have different profiles based on individual style, personality, expectation and life experience. We would like to replicate the work with both younger and older children, where probably both expansion of some elements and modification of others would be necessary. However, in examining all our tran-

Table 16.2 Function Analysis: Fund raising A

	Teacher	Jennifer	Natasha	Robert	Simon
Narration	eee				
Explanation	√	√	√√√	√	√√
Justification	√√			√	
Description	√√√√√	√			
Instruction	√√√√√√ √√	√√√√√	√√√√√√√	√√√√√√√ √√	√ √√√√√√√ √
Information	eeeeeeeeeeee			eee	
Hypothesis	e √√√	√	√	√√√√√√√ √	√
Argument	e √√√√ eeee	√√√√√√√ √	√√√√√√√ √√√	√√√√√√√ √√√√√√√	√√√√√√√

Table 16.3 Function analysis: Problem solving A

	Simon	Rajinder	Natasha	Andrew	John	Jennifer
Narration	√					
Explanation	√√√					
Justification	√√√√√√					
Description	√√		√√√√√√	√√√√	√√√√√	√√√
Instruction			√√	√√√√√√	√√√	√√√√√√
				√√√		√√√√√
Information	√		√√	√	√	√
Hypothesis	√√√		√√√	√ e	ee	√√√√√
Argument			√√√	√		√

scripts of this class of ten- and eleven-year-olds and their teacher it would seem that the recommendation of Cox (8.18) for flexible and varied grouping across the curriculum enabled them to experience, try out and develop a wide language repertoire.

Resource materials are currently being developed and trialled. The author would be very interested to hear from teachers who are working along similar lines in their own schools.

References

Department of Education and Science (1987) *Report of the Committee of Enquiry into the Teaching of English* (The Kingman Report). HMSO, London.

Department of Education and Science (1988) *English for Ages 5 to 11* (The Cox Report). HMSO, London.

Jones, P. (1988) *Lipservice: The Story of Talk in Schools*. Open University Press, Milton Keynes.

Maclure, Phillips and Wilkinson (1988). *Oracy Matters*. Open University Press, Milton Keynes.

Smith, F. (1982) *Understanding Reading*. Holt Rhinehart and Winston, New York.

Bibliography

Barnes, D. (1971) *Language, the Learner and the School*, Penguin.

Crystal, D. (1976) *Child Language, Learning and Linguistics*, Edward Arnold.

Crystal, D., Fletcher, P. and Garman, M. (1982) *The Grammatical Analysis of Language Disability*, Edward Arnold.

Dale, P. S. (1976) *Language Development: Structure and Function*, Holt, Rinehart & Winston.

Davies, A. (1975) *Problems of Language and Learning*, Heinemann.

Donaldson, M. (1984) *Children's Minds*, Fontana.

Moyle, D. (1982) *Children's Word*, Basil Blackwell.

Sinclair, J. McH. and Brazil, D. (1982) *Teacher Talk*, Oxford University Press.

Stubbs, M. (1978) *Language, Schools and Classrooms*, Methuen.

Tough, J. (1976) *Listening to Children Talking*, Ward Lock.

Tough, J. (1977) *Talking and Learning*, Ward Lock.
Tough, J. (1979) *Talk for Teaching and Learning*, Ward Lock.
Wells, G. (1985) *Learning through Interaction*, Cambridge University Press.
Wells, G. (1986) *The Meaning Makers*, Hodder & Stoughton.
Wilkinson, A. and Stratta, L. (1974) *The Quality of Listening*, Macmillan Education.

17 Reading and Writing for Information

Sarah Tann and Roger Beard

The Orders, Key Stage 1, for English (Levels 1 and 2 for 5–7 years) became available in June 1989. One major departure from the framework outlined in the Cox Report of November 1988 is the merging of the two separate components for reading. The Attainment Target 1:

the development of the ability to read, understand and respond to all types of writing (9.11)

and Attainment Target 2:

the development of reading and information-retrieval strategies for the purpose of study (9.12)

have been changed for the June 1989 report to Attainment Target 2:

the development of the ability to read, understand and respond to all types of writing, as well as the development of information-retrieval strategies for the purposes of study. (16.21)

This follows the advice from the National Curriculum Council (NCC) who, after consultation, decided that the division of reading into two separate components was 'unhelpful and artificial' and that 'many skills overlapped' (4.11).

In many ways this was a surprising response from the NCC because in recent years a number of research studies have shown that efficient reading for information is not just a by-product of general reading development. As the Bullock Report warned, in 1975, many of us may well need specific teaching to develop more flexible approaches to reading, which are not line-by-line and at a single rate but, instead, may need to be highly selective and adapted to our particular purposes for using the text.

In reviewing the justification for the new merger we need to ask a number of questions:

● What were the unique features of the information retrieval strategies which were identified in the Cox Report?
● What has happened to these features in the subsequent merger, and how valid is the notion that the existence of two separate components for reading is either 'unhelpful' or 'artificial'?

Reading for Information

The programmes of study in the Cox Report suggested promoting 'children's active engagement with texts', whilst the attainment targets identified a number of aspects as ones which pertained to 'reading and information-retrieval strategies for the purposes of study'. These included the awareness of print sources for information purposes, ability to pose questions in order to read purposefully, ability to select and locate relevant sources (using library system, contents, index and other flagging devices), ability to read and understand the different 'discourse structures' found in the genre of non-fiction books, ability to alter the reading strategy (skim, scan) to meet the particular reading purposes, ability to use books effectively to pursue a line of enquiry (without verbatim copying), and ability to evaluate and weigh evidence and argument. All of these abilities would seem to have a particular meaning in the context of 'reading for information'.

In the subsequent merger, what has happened to the information-retrieval targets? In the NCC Report, many of the unique aspects identified in Cox have been amalgamated into composite attainment targets. This has resulted in a reduction in the number of targets focusing on reading for information, though not a reduction in identified features. (However, such amalgamations may pose severe difficulties where attempts to specify pupil progress in terms of composite targets could lead to ambiguity.)

In the Orders, the attainment targets have been slightly clarified. For example, at Level 1, we continue to have 'discuss the content of stories and information books'; at Level 2, 'demonstrate knowledge of the alphabet in using . . . reference books'; at Level 3, purpose, selection and use of information books are specified and combined in the target, 'devise a clear set of reasoned questions in order to select and use appropriately information books . . .'.

However, a number of attainment targets such as 'listen and respond to . . .' (2.v), 'read with increasing confidence . . .' (2.vi), 'use inference . . . (3.iv), and 'understanding of structure . . .' (3.v) explicitly mention stories and poems only and therefore seem themselves to maintain an unhelpful and artificial distinction, by omitting any reference to non-fiction.

It is particularly in the area of non-fiction structures that children, and teachers, frequently need help because it is a less well documented aspect of reading and writing.

Writing for Information

At Key Stage 2 in the second Cox Report (June 1989), it is confirmed that children will be expected to be developing skills so that they can 'organise non-chronological writing in an orderly way' in a variety of forms and for a range of purposes – to plan, to explain, to express attitudes, emotions and opinions, and to entertain. However, there is an unhelpful lack of explication about what characterises an 'orderly way' and therefore little guidance to help teachers 'teach' children to develop their writing for these purposes. The Cox reports categorise writing in terms of a chronological and non-chronological distinction. Certainly, there is a research to suggest there are structural features to distinguish these types of writing, but equally there is evidence to suggest that there are differences between 'story' structures and 'information' text. The reports offered a breakdown and a progression of features which children's story writing can be expected to show (opening, characterisation, events, endings). There is no help in identifying components of orderly non-chronological writing – or chronological writing for information purposes.

There is nothing in the reports to help us decide what does distinguish chronological, non-fictional writing (say, the animal life cycle) in terms of the style of language and how we organise our 'facts'. We might ask, for example, how should we help children to learn how to decide where to begin, what to include, in which order; where to put, for instance, what the animal is called, what it looks like, the function of specific features, how it lives, learns and adapts, how it behaves with its own kind, with other animals and with humans, what problems, issues or solutions are there?

Which bits of information are necessary (to whom), have we got any gaps, how can we judge accuracy, how do we weight point of view?

Are we clear about the distinguishing characteristics of non-chronological, non-fiction text? Besides, how often do we read, or need to write, 'description' or 'explanation' or 'opinions'? Are we more often likely to use a range of these in a single investigation? Are these distinctions also unhelpful and artificial?

If we do employ these categories of text again we might ask how should we organise the text for 'descriptive writing' – from the general to the particular, from the top to the bottom, from west to east, what it is like, what it is for, what it is made of, how it is made, how it changes? In reporting 'a plan' of, for example, how to design a model, should we define the nature and purpose of each of the items required to fulfil that design and explain their relationships (spatial and causal), or, in 'explaining' an aspect of change in local styles of buildings do we recite the materials, features and construction, and describe their nature, place, function and relationships (cause/consequence/positive/negative)?

When presenting opinions in a 'persuasive' context, should we include propositions, alternatives, limitations, exceptions, evidence, consequences, modifications and conclusions?

Information Skills across the Curriculum

Neither of the Cox reports, nor the programmes of study, are helpful in this area. It is difficult for teachers to help children tackle the different structure of non-fiction books, to identify features, or to make use of them in their own writing without further help in these areas. They particularly need practice and encouragement to formulate questions in a wide range of ways in order to sharpen the children's skills in focusing their responses and their modes of investigating.

Lack of such help may well contribute to the problem of 'verbatim copying' which all the documents point out should be avoided, though none suggest how. It could also be argued that the division between reading and recording/writing (or between literacy and graphicacy (Crystal, 1987) which is maintained through the three attainment targets) is artificial because it seems to neglect the support pupils often need in understanding the structures of the non-fiction texts which they read in adopting a range of ways of recording, handling and presenting information. At present this is only referred to in the Writing target which adopts the categories of chronological and non-chronological writing – although there is mention in the programmes of study of the need to present information in alternative graphic forms. If we turn to other areas of the curriculum there is more help. The Mathematics attainment targets on Handling Data (11.12) provide helpful support offered in terms of ways in which children could be encouraged to translate information from the verbal text to the visual or vice versa. The Science Attainment Target 1 provides ideas for planning, data gathering, and testing, using and communicating information which provides useful guidelines for teachers.

Subdivisions of English

To return to the structure of the three attainment targets for English, how valid is the notion that the separation of reading into two components was unhelpful and artificial? At one level all divisions of language are 'artificial', though most would agree that speaking and listening, reading, and writing were acceptable divisions. Yet the NCC has accepted the further division of writing into writing, spelling and handwriting and the sub-division of writing into chronological and non-chronological. Similarly, within reading there is some reference to using fiction as well as non-fiction – even though there could be confusion if these pairs of terms were to be considered synonymous, for much non-fiction writing, such as life cycles or historical accounts, is chronological . . . This latter point is, however, acknowledged in the programmes of study.

More importantly, in both the reading and the writing attainment targets as well as in the programmes of study, there is little detail to guide teachers in the aims, contexts, activities and appraisal for planning a 'line of enquiry', strategies for information retrieval or the constituents of alternative ways of presenting the findings. Given the knowledge that is now available to teachers from recent research on information retrieval, this lack of detail is particularly 'unhelpful'.

These are sound reasons for reminding ourselves about what research has suggested about the different dimensions of reading development. Much of the reading and writing of everyday life, including the reading of these reports themselves (and writing the responses), involves a special kind of efficient study reading and a very particular style of writing. It would be ironic if the National Curriculum failed properly to promote them.

Bibliography

Avann, P. (ed.) (1985) *Teaching Information Skills in the Primary School*. Edward Arnold, London.

Beard, R. (1984) *Children's Writing in the Primary School*. Hodder & Stoughton Educational and UKRA, Sevenoaks and Ormskirk.

Beard, R. (1987) *Developing Reading 3–13*. Hodder & Stoughton Educational, Sevenoaks.

Crystal, D. (1987) *Child Language, Linguistics and Learning*. Edward Arnold, London.

Flood, J. (ed.) (1984) *Promoting Reading Comprehension*. International Reading Association, Newark, Del.

Gillham, B. (ed.) (1986) *The Language of School Subjects*. Heinemann, London.

Hunter-Carsch, M. (ed.) (1989) *The Art of Reading*. Basil Blackwell, Oxford.

Lunzer, E. and Gardner, K. (1984) *Learning from the Written Word*. Oliver & Boyd, Edinburgh.

Stewart Dore, N. (1986) *Writing and Reading to Learn*. Rozele, Australian Primary English Teaching Association.

Tann, C. S. (ed.) (1988) *Developing Topic Work in the Primary School*. Falmer, Basingstoke.

Wray, D. (1985) *Teaching Information Skills through Project Work*. Hodder & Stoughton Educational and UKRA, Sevenoaks and Ormskirk.

18 Lit-oracy: A Technological Breakthrough

David Moseley

Once upon a time there was a technological breakthrough which adults thought was good for children, although it is rarely used in adult settings for learning Russian or other languages with unfamiliar orthographies. It involved printing some text in such a size that sometimes only one letter could be recognised in a single visual fixation. The text was then propelled at about 4 m.p.h. across the field of vision from right to left. At the same time the words were spoken from a strip of tape. The result was to encourage the subject to rely on memory rather than look closely at the moving visual display. Fortunately, the number of words spoken at once was low, so no real demand on working memory was made. The apparatus tended to be used by dynamic instructors who connected plugs and jack plugs and set switches. They radiated enthusiasm and expected their charges to progress.

The National Curriculum proposals for *English for ages 5 to 16* (DES, 1989) make the point that 'since the information on a word-processor or computer screen is visible to several children at once, it can be a vehicle for group discussion and exploration of the language'. In urging English teachers to make fuller use of information technology the authors of *English for ages 5 to 16* refer to word-processing, redrafting, spell checking and the use of databases – but they have not anticipated the greatly extended range of possibilities that has become available with improved speech synthesis. Not only can pupils' own writing more easily form part of the resources for reading (as the National Curriculum proposals advocate), but improved sight recognition and utilisation of sound–symbol correspondence become possible. 'Difficult' words, phrases and sentences can be immediately checked and it is possible to direct attention very precisely to appropriate cues. By first developing oral reading fluency and then fading out speech support, the transition to silent reading 'with sustained concentration' can be facilitated. Pronunciation, stress, intonation and coherence can be studied in an active learning context and linguistic databases can be compiled and accessed (some of which will be especially useful in multi-lingual classrooms). As more powerful computers become available, the combination of high quality speech with text and graphics will have major implications for language learning at all levels.

Recent attempts to improve literacy standards have used people rather than technology, as in paired and shared reading. While word-processing has gained ground in classrooms and electronic mail has made it more exciting to communicate, computers have received relatively little attention as a means of learning to read. Two kinds of program have, however, been widely accepted: adventure game simulations and cloze exercises. Although these activities can be carried out almost as effectively on paper, it is frequently claimed that group interaction is sustained with the program as a focus.

Of course computers are cheaper than mothers' knees (although they cannot replace them!). But it might be suggested that they can be more reliably programmed than parents to pause, prompt and praise and they can introduce variety and fun into repetitive activities. In terms of phonological and linguistic consistency they can outperform teachers. Now that they can articulate clearly and convey meaning with appropriate stress and intonation, they are capable (with teacher support) of raising every child's level of literacy at least to the level of his/her spoken language.

The writer (1986) set out research-based arguments for using computers constructively in improving reading, writing and spelling. Desirable features of reading programs were thought to include:

- teaching children to categorise words by their sounds, developing fluency in word recognition,
- highlighting linguistic patterns and the relationship between speech and print,
- making use of dynamic text displays, and
- avoiding information overload, visual, auditory and linguistic.

Computer speech has been available for some years and is already at a high level of sophistication for some machines. It is likely that the system now under development for the New BBC Micro (Archimedes System) will outperform most and there is no doubt that the capabilities of such high-speed machines in handling print, graphics and speech will open up exciting possibilities for imaginative authors and programmers. However, with existing technology (the old BBC B Micro), reading and speech can now be linked either in new or old existing programs.

Using Wordwise Plus, with its user-friendly editing, text is translated by the Speech System (Computer Concepts, 1985) into a phonetic code which is spoken by the computer. This is then presented by the Read and Speak program (Moseley, 1989) in any of the following formats:

1   Central 'window' presentation: single words (with clauses and sentences spoken to provide contextual support)
2   Window presentation: phrases
3   Page presentation: cumulative, word by word (with clauses and sentences spoken to provide contextual support)
4   Page presentation: cumulative, phrase by phrase
5   Page presentation: cumulative, sentence by sentence

For each of the above formats the text and speech are linked in one of three ways. If automatic presentation is chosen, the word, phrase or sentence appears long enough for the reader to say it (silently or aloud). The computer then speaks it and the text remains on screen for repetition or study. In fluency building the learner may progress from slow to medium to fast. Alternatively, the user may opt for keyboard control of timing or only when wanted. Repetition of the speech is also available if required.

There are, therefore, twenty-five different ways in which the text may be presented (forty-five ways if choice of print size is added into the equation). This provides both for individual differences and for repetition. Pilot experience with the program shows that sustained attention and mastery learning are possible even in children who have previously failed to respond to skilled support teaching. Using the language-experience approach, children have tape-recorded material which is then presented as a Read and Speak program. Alternatively they have generated lists of topic- or subject-related 'words I want to learn', which have made it possible to cope with more academically demanding work. Longer words are sometimes split into syllables (the most natural speech unit), which are dynamically built up on screen with accompanying speech. Using a slightly different program format, phoneme–grapheme correspondence can also be highlighted, with the help of rhyme and context.

With the support of speech, it is possible for beginning readers and for children who find reading difficult to read 'real language': i.e. for the linguistic demands of the text to be commensurate with those of spoken language in quality if not in quantity. Reading schemes which rely on a restricted vocabulary and range of spelling patterns will no longer be needed, as contextual support and interest will facilitate the search for meaning. There will, however, still be a place for the explicit study of sound–symbol correspondence and of spelling patterns, especially in the context of writing and spelling.

Teachers who take advantage of these developments will need to acquire new reading assessment skills in balancing learning load with application in fluency building. They will also need to research optimal paths to mastery for children with different learning styles, taking into account the information-processing and working memory capacities of the learner. Among the options available the following sequences seem promising.

1 *Normal usage for beginning readers*
   (a) Listening to text using automatic medium-speed cumulative word presentation, with clauses and sentences repeated fluently
   (b) Phrase reading with space bar control, repeating harder phrases
   (c) Sentence reading, with speech only when wanted, as confirmation
   (d) Automatic sentence reading, medium speed
   (e) Automatic sentence reading, fast speed

This avoids one of the problems found with paired and shared reading, where insufficient time is allowed for the reader to focus on, see, hear and repeat each word, while remaining alert to the emerging meaning of the sentence and passage. The sequence proceeds from word to phrase to sentence, providing an opportunity for meaning to be organised in progressively larger units. This is likely to be especially valuable for the poorer readers (Beveridge and Edmundson, 1989). When a good grasp of meaning is achieved, the emphasis switches to fluency building, which will facilitate subsequent decoding and comprehension (Lesgold, 1983).

2   *Normal usage for intermediate level readers*
   (a) Listening to text, with automatic fast presentation of sentences
   (b) Phrase reading, with speech only when wanted, as confirmation
   (c) Sentence reading, giving time for silent rehearsal followed by reading aloud with accompanying speech

Here the intention is to model reading aloud at a fluent rate and simultaneously to communicate a global impression of meaning. Greater attention to detail at the phrase level is then encouraged, with rapid silent reading of well-understood sections. Finally, there is practice in reading aloud without hesitation, which is achieved through familiarity with the passage and silent rehearsal.

3   *For readers with slow word-recognition speed*
   (a) Listening to text, with automatic fast presentation of sentences
   (b) Word presentation, with speech only when wanted, to identify known and unknown words
   (c) Window presentation of phrases containing difficult words as 'flash-card' practice – with space bar control and everything spoken
   (d) Window presentation of difficult words as 'flash-card' practice – with automatic presentation at medium speed
   (e) Window automatic presentation of complete text in phrases, medium speed
   (f) Automatic page presentation of complete text in sentence, fast speed

As slow decoding impairs comprehension, this sequence starts in the same way as the previous one with modelling and a global impression of meaning. It then provides a considerable amount of repetition of words which have proved difficult, both in isolation and in phrases. After this the practised elements are re-integrated into the complete text, which is read twice more with increasing pressure for fluency.

4 *For readers who have difficulty in keeping their place*
   (a) Window single word presentation, with speech only when
       wanted
   (b) Page cumulative word presentation, with space bar control
       and everything spoken
   (c) Automatic page cumulative word presentation, fast speed
   (d) Page cumulative phrase presentation, with speech only
       when wanted
   (e) Sentence reading, with space bar control and everything
       spoken

Here we begin with a task which requires no eye movements
and which is self-paced. Eye movement is then introduced in the
next two stages, but there is no chance of losing the place as each
new word appears. Only when the reader is familiar with the text
does the need arise to make a number of fixations to read each
new chunk, first in phrase and then in sentence reading. Research
by Rayner (1983) provides a convincing rationale for the sequence
proposed above.

5 *For readers with limited working memory capacity*
   (a) Listening to text with automatic cumulative phrase presen-
       tation, slow speed
   (b) Single word window 'flash-card' practice of four difficult
       words at a time, progressing from slow to fast
   (c) Window phrase presentation with space bar control,
       repeating speech three times and reading aloud with it
   (d) Sentence reading, with space bar control and speech only
       when wanted
   (e) Automatic sentence reading, medium speed (to allow time
       for rehearsal)

This approach places an emphasis on verbal coding, which is
acknowledged to be a common weakness in children with specific
reading difficulties (Vellutino, 1987). Presenting the text slowly in
phrase units gives time to make use of all available cues, especially
phonological and grammatical ones. There is also time to rehearse,
before reading aloud with the speech. This is followed by practice
of difficult words to a high level of fluency, so that decoding
problems will not interfere with subsequent reading. Further repetition provided overlearning, followed by a mastery check at

sentence level and finally by a fluency check which again allows for rehearsal.

Many other sequences could be devised and tested out. A trial-and-error self-selection approach may, however, prove to be the best of all, provided that the teacher enters into discussion with the reader as to whether and why the formats used proved helpful. This active learning, problem-solving approach involves reflection on and formulation of learning strategies, and depends on a dynamic process of assessment. Assessment ceases to be a matter of judgement by the expert, using surface features of performance (as in conventional miscue analysis). Assessment and target setting are seen as a joint responsibility and are concerned more with cognitive processes and with the development of effective learning styles and strategies.

With Read and Speak programs an apparently complex reading task can be structured so that it becomes achievable. Print and speech are linked more directly than with a book, yet the outcome is, of course, reading the printout to someone else and perhaps using it as a stimulus for further talking, reading or writing. The National Curriculum objectives and programmes of study will be more easily achieved if access to talking computers is facilitated. Everyone will be able to make their own books, based on talk in the classroom. Words, phrases, phonic cues, spelling patterns and other linguistic features will be used and understood as part of the metalanguage of literacy. Furthermore, by generating and editing their own text for computer speech, children will acquire an awareness of speech sounds, intonation and stress which will be of general benefit in the development of spoken and written language.

References

Beveridge, M. and Edmundson, S. (1989) 'Reading strategies of good and poor readers in word and phrase presentation', *Journal of Research in Reading*, **12**, 1–12.

Computer Concepts (1985) *The Speech System*. Computer Concepts, Hemel Hempstead.

Lesgold, A. M. (1983) 'A rationale for computer-based reading instruction' in Wilkinson, A. C. (ed.) *Classroom Computers and Cognitive Science*. Academic Press, New York.

Moseley, D. V. (1986) 'Improving writing and spelling: an overview'. Chapter in Hope, M. (ed.) *The Magic of the Micro*. MEP/ CET, London.

Moseley, D. V. (1989) *Read and Speak Programs*. Space for Learning, Newcastle-upon-Tyne.

Rayner, K. (1983) *Eye Movements in Reading: Perceptual and Linguistic Aspects*. Academic Press, New York.

Vellutino, F. R. (1987) 'Dyslexia', *Scientific American*, **256**, 20–7.

19 Monitoring the Development of Writing

Richard Binns

Introduction

> Writing is not an activity in itself, not simply a skill. What is of the utmost importance in any langugae task is the child who shows through the language and who finds his voice in the act of talking and writing.
>
> *Hand in your Writing*

Recent reports have stressed the importance of all different modes of language (DES 1988a, 1988b). While the emphasis is rightly placed on teaching, some elements of the teaching process often receive scant attention.

This chapter will explore briefly the place of monitoring in helping children to develop written language.

What is Monitoring?

Monitoring means 'keeping track' (Chambers, 1972); in the case of developing written language this is with reference to difficulties found and progress made. This is quite distinct from any assessment carried out in evaluating the achievement of performance in the final production of a written composition. In monitoring, observation and evaluation relate to the teacher's role in guiding the pupil in learning to handle written language as a medium of communication. To explain what happens in monitoring, three further points are now made, concerning the role of the teacher, the function of monitoring, and the object of monitoring.

The teacher, in acting as a monitor, has a role that involves an element of *detection* (Chambers, 1972). This element is illustrated here with an excerpt from *Language and Personal Growth* (Dixon, 1967), where the author comments on how signs of pausing to re-read in the ordinary course of a ten-year-old boy's diary writing reveal attempts to keep the flow of words and ideas going at the same time as building up meaning.

There are places where he has worked to make something exact . . . in describing newts . . . 'I mean the spots on this one were only on the belly' . . . 'a dark yellow ochre.' It is as if he is listening and scanning what he has just said.

Here the reader (teacher) becomes aware of how the pupil is coping with the fact that in written, unlike spoken, language there is no audience to act as a guide. Monitoring supports the advisory role of the teacher in helping pupils learn to gain a 'sense of audience'. This role differs greatly from acting, for example, as a wider audience. Different questions arise. Does the pupil know that written language is variable? Is the pupil aware that loss of meaning may be attributed to the variability of language in the text on the page, unless there is a clear purpose and context? Finally, is the value of 'horizontal' and 'vertical' scanning appreciated in re-focusing on what to say (Beard, 1984)?

The special function of monitoring is exemplified in the intransitive use of the verb 'to monitor': 'to tap on to a communication circuit, usu. in order to ascertain that the transmission is that desired' (Chambers, 1972).

Monitoring permits an insight into the feedback loop which the young writer has to learn to set up in handling written language as a medium of communication, by returning to re-read the text to gain a 'sense of audience'. It is important for monitoring to be unobtrusive so that the teacher does not influence the pupil in checking the text. Thus the conditions of drafting and re-drafting are ideal, as the pupil is reassured that the teacher reads the text, but not unless requested to do so in his presence; whereas the teacher keeps track of difficulty and progress through comparisons between drafts. Consideration is being given currently to surveying the range of approaches adopted by pupils in self-assessment between drafts (Politt, 1989).

The object of monitoring is to provide a basis for making judgements about intervening. If we accept that the development of written language involves the writer in gaining control over ideas, then monitoring is especially important, because it helps the teacher to draw a dividing line between intervening and interfering during composing, when the delicate relationship between thought and language may be upset (Britton et al., 1975, Ch. 2; Binns and Liddell, 1980).

Although the teacher may not be intervening, monitoring is a very active process in which the teacher makes judgements all the time on the basis of observations – judgements which may result in the decision to allow children to continue exploring ideas and using language or to support them in working out what to say or how to proceed.

What does the Teacher Need to be Aware of in Order to Monitor?

In order to monitor the teacher has got to be operating from a background of knowledge and understanding of the many factors that may come into play during the development of written language – audience, context, use of time and space.

The teacher needs criteria on which judgements can be made as to where the child is. These criteria are generally held to fall into two categories: aspects of development in composing, and factors affecting the writing process. In discussing these criteria references to the literature included here relate in particular to recent research policy development and practices in Scottish schools. The latter references share three common factors.

1   Writing is seen as a reflective act.
2   Guidance may take place early in the composing process – at the stage of planning and rehearsing what to say – rather than at the final stage of composition, when advice may be related to proof reading and revising to check the acceptability of a passage in terms of the accepted conventions.
3   Self-assessment by pupils.
    (a) With reference to aspects of development in composing, this may involve appreciation of the extent to which objectives have been met (thus dealing with content, organisation and mechanics).
    (b) In terms of the factors affecting development, there may be a growing awareness of the importance of making use of the opportunity to pause to re-read what has been

written, as a guide to the text (revision, as distinct from revising).

Three aspects of development are now considered: purpose, audience, context. A purpose for writing is generally held to be essential. What is not so widely recognised is the fact that writers benefit from returning to the text to gain a greater sense of purpose through reading over their work. For example, digression or break-down of the flow of words and ideas may indicate not so much inability to organise as the necessity to return to the text for greater involvement. In consequence of time for internal debate about what to say, 'delay' for reflection may lead to the emergence of clarification and/or development of meaning (Binns, 1978, 1980).

'Audience' refers in most instances to the wider readership for writing. Awareness of the reader's expectations is very important to the young writer in learning to adopt a particular point of view. The term 'sense of audience' refers on the other hand to the writing process when the writer pauses to review what to say or how to proceed (CCC/COPE, 1982; Binns, 1988). In the latter connection, the act of 'valuing' the text is critical (Graves, 1983, Ch. 15). Valuing occurs when the writer becomes involved in responding to different parts of the text on the page in order to weigh up content, effectiveness of the use of language, the direction to take in re-organising or re-shaping.

A sense of context is vital in weighing up a passage in terms of purpose and audience. 'Success in writing' may serve either before or after drafting as a 'model' for internalising 'standards' in terms of the effective use of language in a particular context (Peacock, 1986). Awareness of context as the determinant of meaning may also be a matter for consideration in evaluating where a child is even at beginning to realise the value of checking the surface structure of the text against the intended meaning to see the direction to take in re-writing (CCC/COPE, 1986, Ch. 2).

It is evident from the preceding references to aspects of develop-ment that it is important to take into consideration in monitoring the various factors affecting the writing process. Three factors are now referred to: use of time and space; the teacher's response; and the pupil's response.

Appreciation of the use of 'time and space' is vital, if children are to handle written language as a medium of communication (Smith, 1982). This factor of time and space is linked by Smith to the notion of the 'writer as reader' – reader of his or her own work before a wider audience. Smith stresses the value of time to review and specify 'intentions'.

The teacher's response depends in monitoring on 'sensitivity' within a clear framework of criteria that combines an appreciation of the pupil's 'stance' in writing for a particular purpose and audience with a grasp of the 'characteristics of writing' – 'selection, explicitness, coherence, structure, conventions' (CCC/COPE, 1982). A practical illustration of the teacher's response in the form of 'interior monologue' is illuminating, especially when an attempt is made to strike a balance between different reasons for intervening (CCC/COPE, 1986).

The pupil's response to writing may be influenced by the frustration of handling written language as a medium of communication, especially in not being able to get ideas down first time. Slips, errors and 'false starts' may be attributed generally to the time taken to pause for reflection in the ordinary course of writing (Goldman-Eisler in Britton et al., 1975). Seeing 'where the failure to write may lie' may relieve pupils' frustration; for example, through either reducing insistence on correctness on the 'surface aspects of written language' or explaining about 'differences between spoken and written language' (CCC/COPE, 1982).

Monitoring – Then What?

There is no question that monitoring is an essential part of the on-going responsibilities of the class teacher. The issue is how to monitor most effectively since monitoring offers the possibility of making a more informed judgement in providing guidance for pupils learning to write better. Care in monitoring the steps taken by children in completing a piece of individual or shared writing assists formative evaluation of the individual child's progress and can increase understanding of the writing process itself. The further question may then be asked, can anything be done about looking into the nature of difficulty and progress in handling written language as a medium of communication? Although we cannot see into the writer's mind to observe either what aspect of development may be of concern or what might be the sticking point in the writing process, there is the opportunity of noting a difficulty and evaluating on a further occasion of writing the possible factors affecting the writer's ability to re-read, pause for reflection and re-write. Monitoring between drafts affords the opportunities to look more closely into an individual's strengths and weaknesses as a writer.

To summarise: monitoring as one on-going aspect of formative assessment has two complementary sides, prescriptive and diagnostic.

Monitoring – Where To?

In Scotland, the need for 'the evaluation and assessment of written work' was reported in a survey (Spencer et al., 1983) and discussed (Spencer, 1983): 'There was little evidence of any major effort to develop or explain the skills and strategies with which pupils could approach the particular problem of the writing they were to do.'

Since then, the Consultative Committee on the Curriculum and the Committee on Primary Education have brought out advisory documents to assist teachers in responding to children's written language.

In England, the National Writing Project has fostered widespread interest in exploring the process of encouraging children to 'behave as writers' (Czerniewska, 1989; Hall, 1989). A wealth of evidence has accrued of teachers following closely their pupils' development as writers. For example, an unobtrusive approach to monitoring (Hall, 1989) reveals through an exchange of letters 'the emergence of authorship' during the early years of the primary school in such aspects of development as the 'choice' to 'maintain' or 'expand' topics to 'generate or to introduce a completely new topic'; also in 'handling more than one topic'. These results raise important issues. Can we expect pupils to develop as writers from an earlier age than previously recognised as a direct result of 'developing writing'? How should support be varied at different ages to deal with different kinds of difficulty in handling written language? Some partial answers to these questions may be found in the descriptions of children in the classroom at work as writers; creating an environment through modelling, drawing and talking to encourage pupils to 'anticipate writing' (Jackson and Michael, 1987) or ensuring pupils are able to conceptualise a topic (Graves, 1983)?

In the classroom, monitoring is invaluable in helping teachers to meet the attainment targets recommended for Writing in the

Cox Report that stresses in particular the ability 'to construct and convey meanings in written language'. This is given the possibility that programmes of study permit the integration of drafting and re-drafting and its related opportunities for monitoring into classwork. This possibility is endorsed in the recent review referred to above, 'The Curriculum Council's considered view of the Cox Report'.

Welcome additions to the programmes of study include a five element model of the writing process: decision-making; planning; drafting; presentation and evaluation, though it's unfortunate that drafting is reduced to fair-copy production; 'working towards clear, grammatically accurate text' rather than working towards a text that is effective given its audience and purpose.

(Czerniewska, 1989)

In order to meet children's special needs it is essential to monitor their way of working. This is exemplified in general in helping with 'spelling and meaning' (CCC/COPE, 1986). More particularly, helping children with difficulties in writing in returning to re-read the text as an aid to visualising what to say is vital (McLullich and Palmer, 1988). In addition, linguistic awareness may be observed in re-reading to check (with the aid of a code of symbols) the text's intended meaning (Binns, 1980). Thus what goes on in the course of monitoring may reassure the teacher about such essential matters as how best to assist children to learn the conventions of written English including copy with genre register, spelling and grammar.

Conclusion

While it is clear that the role of the teacher in developing children's speaking, listening, reading and writing is crucial, the significance of the monitoring process within that cannot be overstated.

References

Beard, R. (1984) *Children's Writing in the Primary School*. Hodder and Stoughton, Sevenoaks.

Binns, R. (1978) *From Speech to Writing*. Centre for Information for the Teaching of English/Scottish Curriculum Development Service, Moray House College of Education, Edinburgh Centre.

Binns, R. (1980) 'A Technique for Developing Written Language' in Clark, M. M. and Glynn, T. (eds), *Reading and Writing for the Child with Difficulties*. Education Review, Occasional Publication No. 8, University of Birmingham.

Binns, R. (1988) 'Re-creation through Writing' in Hunter-Carsch, M. (ed.) *The Art of Reading*. Blackwell Education, Oxford.

Binns, R. and Liddell, G. (1980) *Teaching Writing with Slower Learners – a dialogue concerning intervention*. Scottish Curriculum Development Service, Moray House College of Education, Edinburgh Centre.

Britton, J. et al. (1975) *The Development of Writing Abilities, 11–18*. Macmillan.

Chambers Twentieth Century Dictionary (1972).

Consultative Committee on the Curriculum/Committee on Primary Education in Scotland (1982) *Hand in your Writing*.

Consultative Committee on the Curriculum/Committee on Primary Education in Scotland (1986) *Responding to Children's Writing*. Development Group on Language Arts of the Scottish Committee on Language Arts in the Primary School.

Czerniewska, P. (1988) 'The National Writing Project: Thoughts about the Early Years' in Hunter-Carsch, M. (ed.) *The Art of Reading*. Blackwell Education, Oxford.

Czerniewska, P. (1989) 'Pam Czerniewska looks at the Curriculum Council's considered view of the Cox Report'. *Times Educational Supplement*.

Department of Education and Science (1988a) *Report of the Committee of Enquiry into the Teaching of English* (The Kingman Report). HMSO, London.

Department of Education and Science (1988b) *English for Ages 5 to 11*. (The Cox Report). HMSO, London.

Dixon, J. (1967) 'Language and Personal Growth' in Larson, R. L. (1975) *Children and Writing in the Primary School*. Oxford University Press, Oxford.

Graves, D. H. (1983) *Writing – Teachers and Children at Work*. Heinemann, London.

Hall, N. (ed.) (1989) *Writing with Reasons*. Hodder and Stoughton, Sevenoaks.

Jackson, W. J. and Michael, B. (1987) *Foundations of Writing Project*. Consultative Committee on the Curriculum/Committee on Primary Education in Scotland, Moray House College of Education, Edinburgh.

McLullich, H. and Palmer, S. (1988) 'The Inward Eye: A Personal Investigation of Mental Imagery' in Hunter-Carsch, M. (ed.) *The Art of Reading*. Blackwell Education.

Peacock, C. (1986) *Teaching Writing*. Croom Helm.

Politt, A. (1989) *English Language Monitoring Project* (in progress).

Smith, F. (1982) *Writing and the Writer*. Heinemann Educational Books.

Spencer, E. (1983) *Writing Matters across the Curriculum*. Hodder and Stoughton for the Scottish Council for Research in Education.

Spencer, E. et al. (1983) *Written Work in Scottish Secondary Schools*. Scottish Council for Research in Education.

20 English: Assessment and Record Keeping

Bridie Raban

A framework for national assessment

Assessment, as defined by the Task Group on Assessment and Testing (TGAT) report (DES/WO, 1988), may be any procedure, formal or informal, for producing information about pupils. This need for information about pupils is central to the implementation and purpose of the National Curriculum (Education Reform Act, 1988) and provides a sharp focus for recording and interpreting observations of pupil progress already made by teachers in busy classrooms. Naturally, there are fears that a programme of assessment which requires public scrutiny for all 7- and 11-year-olds in primary schools will increase the workload on teachers to an extreme degree. This of course would be the case if assessment is to be viewed as an additional activity for teachers. However, close reading of the TGAT report clearly allays this fear. It is valuable, therefore, to keep a clear picture in mind of the major points made by the report and in view of the model of assessment put forward, find an appropriate role for assessment which needs to be seen as an integral part of both teaching and learning.

The TGAT report stresses that the assessment process itself should not determine what is to be taught and learnt. It should be part of the educational process, continually providing teachers with feedback on the success of their teaching strategies and information for future teaching plans. In view of this, teachers' records and assessments over time and in normal contexts play an important part, and methods of assessment may often be incorporated into normal classroom activities. The TGAT working group acknowledged that teachers typically use a wide range of sources to provide information for assessment; general impressions, marking class work, pupils' self-assessment, rating scales, check lists, practical and written tests. The national system of assessment they propose will be a combination of teachers' own records and assessment results together with the results of Standard Assessment Tasks (SATs).

SATs are being developed and will be administered nationally at the four reporting age points. Their purpose is to supplement the continuous records of and assessment of teachers in order to give an overall indication of pupil standards and progress through the National Curriculum. These externally provided assessment methods and procedures will be broad in scope and relate to the curriculum attainment targets which all pupils will share. SATs, therefore, are being developed in a broader framework than traditional test instruments. Their range and scope will be much wider than a mere reading age test, for instance. SATs will be presented to pupils and responded to by them in a variety of ways; pupils' activities need not be written responses only. In particular, they must be designed to achieve educational validity, they must measure what they set out to measure in relation to a wide range of learning aims. Therefore, there should not need to be a sharp discontinuity between teacher assessment and SATs. Indeed, pupils need not be aware of any departure from normal classroom work. This is stressed in the report with regard especially to the youngest age group.

The TGAT report, therefore, provides a broadly based framework for assessment which puts teachers at the centre of the process. The associated moderation procedures which bring groups of teachers together will provide a forum for producing the agreed combination of moderated teacher ratings and the results of SATs. Assessment procedures, at whatever level of formality, can only be useful in so far as they reflect the achievements of pupils; the closer these procedures are to everyday classroom activities, the more valid their results will be.

Assessment in the National Curriculum is required to fulfil four main purposes; formative, diagnostic, summative and evaluative. National assessment at the first stage (7 years) will be aimed primarily at identifying pupils in need of help and will serve a diagnostic and evaluative purpose. Formative information collected at each key stage will be used to plan future work with pupils and only at the final key stage (16 years) does the assessment become summative. The formative aspect of assessment calls for appropriate profile reporting and the exercise of professional judgement on the part of teachers.

Development and Assessment in English

The English working group (DES/WO, 1989a) used these recommendations from the TGAT report to guide their own thinking on assessment in English. They acknowledge the inappropriateness of defining language development as a linear sequence. They stress that language development is a process of refining competence as different aspects are returned to time and again with increasing sophistication. However, within this model of spiralling progress, it is still possible to have expectations of pupil competencies at certain stages of schooling; for instance, when pupils change schools from infant to junior and on to secondary stage, when forms of teaching and teachers alter and new courses of work lie ahead. These are traditionally the occasions when teachers report to each other and parents concerning the competencies and progress of pupils. In view of this, they argue that the requirements for national assessment at key stages makes current good practice both more explicit and common across all schools.

The English curriculum is now defined by profile components which are made up of attainment targets. These attainment targets are defined in their turn by ten levels of attainment described by statements of attainment. Their relationship is shown in Table 20.1.

Table 20.1

Profile Component	Attainment Targets	Statements of Attainment
Speaking and Listening	1 Speaking and Listening	Levels 1–10
Reading	2 Reading	Levels 1–10
Writing	3 Writing	Levels 1–10
	4 Spelling	Levels 1–4
	5 Handwriting	Levels 1–4
	4/5 Presentation	Levels 5–7

The way in which the profile components and attainment targets in English have been identified takes maximum advantage of the possibility for assessing pupil progress across the full range of primary classroom activities. Speaking and listening, reading, writing, spelling and handwriting all have a place throughout the integrated curriculum which characterises the best of primary practice. These curricular opportunities for observing learning in English act as additional and supporting information to those records kept of progress through the English curriculum itself. In this way, needless duplication of records can be avoided. Indeed, the English working group stress that spoken and written language competence is dependent on context with the implication that pupil responses to the widest range of tasks and variety of contexts will be required to achieve an adequate record of progress and accurate assessment when this is required. It is also stressed that forms of record keeping and assessment must pay attention to the process of accomplishing different activities using language as well as the product of these events.

While the English working group agreed with TGAT's rough estimate of median levels of attainment at each key stage, they argued for a wider range of attainment around the median than TGAT proposed. They acknowledge that the learning process in English is characterised both by high and low levels of attainment unlike other content-based subjects. Therefore, they recommend a wider range of levels associated with each key stage (Table 20.2).

Table 20.2

Key Stage	Age (years)	Median attainment	Range of attainment
1	7	Level 2	Levels 1–3
2	11	Level 4	Levels 2–5
3	14	Levels 5/6	Levels 3–8
4	16	Levels 6/7	Levels 3–10

Teacher Assessment and SATs

Standard Assessment Tasks will be the form of the external assessment requirements for reporting on pupil progress in the national curriculum at each key stage. They are presently being designed to provide teachers with a package of different activities for them to choose from which arise out of familiar classroom contexts. They will cover a variety of forms of presentation and require a range of pupil responses. More importantly, they can be conducted over an extended period of time rather than be confined to a short timed exercise. This form of assessment will be standard for all pupils at the reporting ages which will be needed to provide bench marks across schools and LEAs. Their results will, however, be taken in the light of more detailed and continuous assessments which teachers make of individual pupils in the process of their normal observations and record keeping.

External assessment will be built on an extended SAT. These tasks will be based on a classroom project and will sample spoken and written language behaviours in a variety of contexts. For 7-year-olds, pupil responses to a range of presentations will be both individual and group, mainly oral and practical, although written and graphical responses will also be sampled appropriately. At 11 years of age, greater weight will be given to written responses and individual activities. Schools and teachers will have a choice from alternative SATs; in this way they will be able to ensure that the activities match best the content of their classroom work.

The assessment of speaking and listening, in particular, should be informal, continuous and incidental and applied to tasks carried out for a wide variety of curricular purposes. Although the Cox Report does not recommend the use of tape-recorders for individual pupil's oral performance, it is clearly not possible to moderate assessment results within this profile component without such evidence. The English working group have probably underestimated the use of tape-recorders in primary classrooms and could well encourage teachers to use them in a more planned and structured way to support the need for assessment of oral language. The National Oracy Project is having an increasingly positive impact on this area of teachers' work. Examples of pupils' talk in a wide variety of contexts for many different purposes are giving guidance for more accurate observation as well as increasing the repertoire of teachers' skills for generating and sustaining talk in classrooms.

External assessment of reading will cover reading comprehension, thus focusing on the result of reading rather than any performance aspect of the process. Activities already available through the Assessment of Performance Unit (1988) and Vincent and de la Mare (1986) give indications of what to expect. Texts will need to be coherent and relevant to the classroom experiences of pupils. Again, at age 7 years, responses will be mainly oral and at age 11 there will be greater emphasis on written responses. For Writing, teachers of pupils at age 7 will be expected to provide three contrasting pieces: a short narrative based on personal experience, a poem, and a list or a factual account based on observation. These pieces will provide evidence for assessing all the attainment targets ensuring that spelling and handwriting are not separately assessed out of context. In addition, at age 11, two short, timed writing tasks will be required.

Internal assessment requirements for the national curriculum will be based on those used by individual teachers and schools which centre on day-to-day record keeping. This is the hallmark of informed primary practice. These procedures are both planned and structured to reflect the content of the English curriculum and its progression now through levels of attainment. In order that this criterion is met, the assessment element of record keeping will now need to be discussed and moderated with colleagues both within the same school and elsewhere. An example of this kind of record-keeping is suggested by the English working group. They have identified the Primary Language Record (PLR, Barrs, 1988) as a valuable starting point of teachers who are beginning to make their own records reflect the profile components of the English curriculum and who now need to make their observations more explicit and available for other teachers and parents. In order to standardise internal assessments, Schools Examination and Assessment Council (SEAC) will be developing a common national format.

It would be highly inappropriate for teachers to take over a publicly available form of record keeping like PLR mentioned above without opportunities for substantial discussion and in-service support. The best record-keeping formats are those devised by teachers working together locally who can fine-tune their procedures to their own pupils and relevant needs in relation to the curriculum objectives which are now becoming nationally available. This, of course, is how PLR was developed and provides a useful discussion document for any re-evaluation or modification which is felt necessary to individual schools' current practice. Records of pupil observations and ways of interpreting these for assessment purposes are so inextricably bound up with the general processes of teaching and learning that they cannot be added on after decisions have been made about implementing the curriculum. Forms of record keeping will be a natural part of the discussions around programmes of study and schemes of work.

The variety of ways in which pupils use spoken language for learning will require teachers to keep records of both verbatim responses and behaviours in relation to talk. While general guidance is available for this continuous process, a common format has yet to be devised by SEAC. Common national formats for record keeping and pupils' self-assessment will also be devised for reading and writing. Teachers' structured observations should seek to identify pupils' growing confidence and independence as readers and writers.

Records of continuous assessment in reading will cover what has been read, reading strategies and approaches to familiar texts, levels of comprehension, retrieval of information and reading tastes and preferences. Miscue analysis will play a central part in identifying strategies and approaches to text as well as assessing comprehension. More importantly, techniques like this reveal profiles of strengths and weaknesses and differentiate between varieties of errors. In writing, internal assessment will focus mainly on the writing process as distinct from the product. This will require records of pupils' conferences where ideas for writing and drafts are discussed. Also samples of work at different stages of the process will need to be collected alongside finished pieces. In particular, pupils' ability to reflect on what they are doing will provide valuable information concerning their growing confidence and independence.

There is a danger that weak forms of internal assessment will give undue prominence to the results of SATs and this is to be avoided. It is only through the structured observations of teachers and their dated records of language events across a wide range of tasks and contexts that SAT results can be modified accurately to assess the attainment levels of individual pupils. When there is a discrepancy between the results of external and internal forms of assessment, the TGAT report comes down on the side of internal assessment. However, if the bases of these internal assessments are not sufficiently detailed and clearly structured to resolve the discrepancy unequivocally, then the results of SATs will be taken as final. Indeed, SEAC is making moves towards this possibility

(Nash, 1989) and it is, therefore, a matter of some urgency that teachers' own record keeping and forms of internal assessment survive positive public scrutiny in the immediate future.

Reporting Levels of Attainment

The English curriculum is now defined by levels of attainment which are made up of statements which identify strands which run through the levels. A pupil achieves a level of attainment if all the strands in that level have been achieved. However, a pupil may be making progress with some of the strands in the following levels and these should be noted. Individual strengths and weaknesses will become clearer if this amount of detail in records is retained and will be particularly valuable information for sharing with other teachers planning future work and for reporting to parents (Table 20.3).

The kinds of information shared with parents and other teachers will be very different from those made available concerning a school or LEA. Public scrutiny beyond the immediate context of the school and classroom will not be of sufficient detail to reveal the achievements of individual pupils. More importantly, all documents concerning the National Curriculum accept that there will be a period of time while both the curriculum and these assessment procedures are tried in practice. The curriculum itself may well over- or underestimate the progress which can be expected of pupils at different ages and only time and continuous monitoring will reveal any discrepancies which require modifications. The most essential evidence for these modifications will be teachers' continuous records of dated observations including samples of pupils' work across time. This kind of evidence will be the major

Table 20.3

Reporting to parents	*School or LEA profiles*
Level achieved for each individual attainment target and strands achieved at higher levels	Single score for English equally weighted for Key Stages 1 and 2 Aggregation of levels across profile components (% of pupils at each level to be reported)

indication of the appropriate rates of development and progress.

Guidelines for the accumulation of evidence are given in the non-statutory guidance (DES/WO, 1989b) now available in all schools. The chart on page D2 gives a clear indication of what this evidence might look like. The three main areas of data collection for records are factual details, teachers' observations and samples of work. These would best be collected under the headings of the five attainment targets rather than the three profile components as set out in the chart, although spelling and handwriting should never be assessed apart from more general writing purposes. Further records will need to be kept of conferences with individual pupils and their self-assessments along with notes of discussions with parents. Cumulatively, these records will serve all the necessary purposes of assessment:

- help in planning further work
- feedback and response for pupils themselves
- curriculum coverage maintained
- information for other teachers
- evidence for assessment at reporting ages

This programme of assessment and its inter-relatedness with teaching and learning provides a challenge for all members of the profession. There is much that needs to be done in order to achieve its design in both principle and practice. That it will take place, there can be no doubt. What remains important is that classroom teachers continue to provide the evidence both for establishing appropriate criteria for judging pupil progress and for designing the classroom-based procedures which do not divert them significantly from their main purpose of teaching and pupil learning.

References

Assessment of Performance Unit (1988) *Assessing Reading: Pupils aged 11 and 15 years*. NFER-Nelson.

Barrs, M. (1988) *Primary Language Record*. Inner London Education Authority.

Department of Education and Science/Welsh Office (1988) *National Curriculum – Task Group on Assessment and Testing: A Report*. HMSO.

Department of Education/Welsh Office (1989a) *English for ages 5 to 16.* HMSO.

Department of Education/Welsh Office (1989b) *English in the National Curriculum.* HMSO.

The Education Reform Act (1988).

Nash, I. (1989) 'Unlikely to accept coming second in endurance test'. *Times Educational Supplement,* 4 August, p. 8.

Vincent, D. and de la Mare, M. (1986) *Effective Reading Test.* Macmillan.

21 Special Educational Needs and the National Curriculum

Sue Beverton and Alan Dyson

A remarkable omission from the Government's initial proposals on the National Curriculum (DES, 1987) was any significant attempt to take account of the curricular requirements of children with special needs. Uncharitable commentators were heard to say that the Government had simply forgotten about the Warnock 'one-in-five' (DES, 1978). Although subsequent documents from the National Curriculum Council and the DES have gone some way to remedy this situation, we are left with a strong sense that the decision to include children with special needs was very much an afterthought. Nonetheless, we hold that the consequences of this omission or lack of attention may paradoxically be to bring benefits to special needs teaching and pupils.

What is the National Curriculum?

This simple question has far-reaching implications.

1 The National Curriculum is a common curriculum

As the National Curriculum Council say: the principle that all pupils should have access to a broad and balanced curriculum is now for the first time established in law (NCC Circular No. 5).

This marks a radical change for pupils with special needs. In this post-Warnock era, we are used to offering such children an alternative curriculum. Indeed, the Warnock Report (1978) sanctions a 'modified curriculum' as one of the three principle strategies available to special needs educators. This might mean simply an hour's remedial reading per week or, at the other extreme, an entirely different curriculum such as the developmental curricula of some special schools.

Now it is, quite literally, illegal to run such alternative curricula. They contravene the principle of a common curriculum, whose structure, content and, to a certain extent, delivery style are laid down in statutory orders having the force of law. The implication is that special needs provision will have to operate within the mainstream curriculum, not outside it.

2 The National Curriculum is accessible to all

Considerable care has been taken by the National Curriculum Council to ensure that there are no entry requirements. The majority of attainment targets, for instance, have been written so that sensorily handicapped pupils can work towards them without modification. Level 1 targets in particular have been designed so that *all* children, including those with profound and multiple handicaps, can make a start on a common curriculum. Thus there is no need to separate children with special needs in order to 'prepare' them prior to participation in that curriculum. Interestingly, the same notion of accessibility without reference to attainment is apparent in the Non-Statutory Guidelines for English Key Stage 1, where part of the definition of a scheme of work is that it 'should reflect whole-school approaches to teaching and learning as part of the continuum from pre-school age to the age of 16' (DES, 1989, p. B1).

The logic is remarkably simple: because the curriculum is common to all children, the underlying processes of teaching and learning are common to all. Furthermore, as those processes are common, access to them is a particularly significant consequence with regard to English in this absence of entry requirements. English now ceases to hold a pivotal position within the curriculum. Hitherto certain English skills, particularly in the area of so-called basic literacy, were often held to be a pre-requisite for access to other curricular areas. Now, however much English is valued in its own right as a core subject, the fact is that pupils' access to *other* areas of the curriculum need no longer depend so crucially upon literacy skills and abilities.

There are implications here for those working in the field of meeting special educational needs. Just one example might be that local education authority services calling themselves Literacy Support ('Remedial Reading') Services or whatever, which used to concentrate on restricted areas of, say, the reading process, will now have to reconsider their roles and areas of responsibility. In our view there is no longer the justification for the exclusive bond between English and special needs work – a circumstance about which we shall say more below.

3 The National Curriculum offers a structured teaching programme and makes possible the assessment of pupils' progress through that programme

The dominant form of assessment in special needs education has tended to be both *psychometric* and *diagnostic*. Special needs teachers, often with the 'expert' assistance of educational psychologists, have sought to measure children's fundamental abilities and learning characteristics in order to arrive at 'diagnoses' of children's difficulties. These diagnoses were intended to lead to appropriate remedial programmes, or, where remediation was posisble, to appropriately modified curricula.

The National Curriculum, however, implies a *curriculum-based* model of assessment. The principal thrust of this assessment – despite certain qualifications in the Task Group on Assessment and Testing Report (DES, 1987) – is towards what the children can do at a particular point in time with regard to a given set of curricular objectives. In other words the thrust is towards children's attainments on the various attainment targets. Once a child's current levels of attainment are known, the teacher also knows in which direction subsequent teaching should follow and thus which statements of attainment will subsequently be tackled.

There is no question in all this, as far as we can see, of assessing underlying abilities or long-term learning difficulties, because such information is simply irrelevant to the task in hand. Even where the assessment process outlined above does not yield sufficient information to enable the teacher to determine what to teach next, all that may be needed is more of the same – assessment of finer gradation of attainment.

Implications for special needs teaching

These three characteristics of the National Curriculum seem to us to imply a re-definition of what special needs work is about. Traditionally we are accustomed to special needs education as seeming more or less distinct from the delivery of the 'mainstream' curriculum. We have conceptualised it in terms of either the teaching of 'modified' curricula or of remediation programmes. Both forms are seen as distinct from and, in the latter case especially, preparatory to, the mainstream curriculum.

However, the National Curriculum, as a common, and commonly accessible, curriculum implies, it seems to us, that the only legitimate concern of *all* teachers is the effective delivery of that curriculum to *all* pupils. The corollary of this is that special needs teachers can no longer function in 'splendid isolation' with concerns that are separate from those of their mainstream colleagues. Special needs teachers must henceforth engage with the question of how the least able and most disadvantaged children can participate in *common* learning experiences.

There is, of course, a considerable body of good practice in terms of how special needs teachers can involve themselves in the mainstream classroom. Support teaching and whole-school approaches to special needs have done much to break down the barriers. Yet it is essential not to confuse the effective delivery of a common curriculum with the simple physical placement of special needs pupils and teachers in mainstream lessons. There is a growing body of evidence (Hart, 1986; Gipps and Gross, 1987; Bines, 1986, 1988) that such placement can lead to a little more than the delivery of traditional remedial teaching in a different context.

The crucial question therefore is not *where* a pupil is taught but *how* s/he is taught, and whether the learning experiences with which the pupil is provided actually amount to access to the common curriculum. We would argue that the skills which special needs teachers have developed in assessing individuals' learning abilities need to be extended so that they encompass the assessment of the effectiveness of learning situations and the devising of increasingly effective methods of curriculum delivery.

Many special needs teachers have, for instance, an intuitive understanding, based on wide experience, of how particular children respond to particular teaching approaches. They also have specific skills in assessing certain areas of learning situations, such as the readability of texts. These skills can and should be further developed and applied, through the use in particular of structured observation, to the systematic assessment of the key elements in the learning situation, such as task, teaching style, peer group influences, seating arrangements and so on. Similarly, many special needs teachers are able to assess fine gradations of learning in specific curricular areas. They are, for instance, accustomed, in listening to children read, to assessing what the children have learned, what needs to be learnt next and how that might be taught. Such skills are equally applicable in other curricular areas. A similarly attentive and aware style of listening is equally valuable in assessing a child's understanding of scientific concepts or in helping a child work out the next stage of his/her design project.

However, the development and application of techniques such as these is not in itself sufficient. Assessment of learning situations can only take place within those learning situations – that is, in mainstream classrooms. Moreover, any changes in practice which that assessment suggests can only be implemented by mainstream teachers. It is essential, therefore, that special needs teachers develop skills in working collaboratively with mainstream colleagues. This implies that the special needs teacher must resist the temptation to fulfil the traditional role of 'sole provider' for particular children, and must be prepared to adopt a consultative role. This will not happen without careful planning, and while many models of consultancy work are available (see, for instance, Gray, 1988), we would suggest that the following steps might be well worth considering.

1 The special needs teacher should carry out a personal skills inventory, identifying clearly skills which s/he possesses that are already relevant or could be enhanced to become relevant to the new role. S/he should also identify key areas in which new skills need to be developed so that this need can be fed into the school's or service's staff development programme.

2 The special needs teacher, in collaboration with mainstream colleagues, should identify points at which effective delivery of the curriculum to pupils with special needs is likely to prove difficult, given existing teaching practice.

3 The special needs teacher, in collaboration with mainstream colleagues, should identify the contribution s/he can make to the overcoming of these difficulties. While this contribution may well be in terms of the direct teaching of certain children, s/he should bear in mind that it is simply not possible to provide 'support' to every deserving child in every curriculum area, and that short-term interventions, structured assessments, and the collaborative formulation of teaching and learning

programmes may well be a more effective and efficient use of a finite time resource.

4 The special needs teacher, in collaboration with mainstream colleagues, should endeavour to turn these general commitments into precise statements of what is to be done, by whom, with what objectives, for how long, and with what procedures for monitoring and evaluation. These statements may well take the form of contracts, written or otherwise, and will amount to a detailed description of the special needs teacher's role together with a means of evaluating his/her effectiveness.

English and Special Needs Teaching

We have thus far deliberately avoided any emphasis on the place of English in the redefined role of the special needs teacher. It is our view, stated above, that the almost exclusive bond between much special needs work and English, interpreted narrowly as certain literacy skills, is seriously challenged by the National Curriculum. Nonetheless, it is becoming apparent from both statutory and non-statutory curriculum documents (the non-statutory guidance on Science (DES, 1989) is perhaps clearest in this respect) that there is a range of skills which are fundamental to the whole curriculum. They are fundamental in two senses: first, they are to be taught, it would appear, through the medium of many if not all subjects, and in this sense are cross-curricular; second, they are skills which, as they are learned, themselves facilitate further learning, and thus become the cognitive keys which unlock the various subject areas. These skills are in such areas as problem solving, designing and carrying out investigations, target setting and self-monitoring, participation in collaborative work, and information access, management, and communication. The traditional 'basic literacy' skills certainly comprise one element in this range, but the part they play, while significant, is limited.

If pupils are to become effective learners, it is essential that these skills are taught effectively. Any failure by the school in this respect is doubly handicapping in that it limits not only what pupils know, but also what they can go on to learn. It would seem that effective teaching of these cross-curricular skills is likely to require a high degree of curriculum co-ordination, particularly in respect of special needs pupils, whose ability to learn from incidental experience or to generalise from one curriculum area to another might in some cases be restricted.

The special needs teacher, playing the broader role outlined above, will in many schools be in a unique position to work for the necessary degree of co-ordination. By collaborating with a range of mainstream colleagues, and by focusing on effective teaching and learning, s/he can do much to ensure the delivery of a coherent programme of skills teaching to each pupil. Indeed, some special needs teachers might wish to see this whole area of learning skills as an area of particular expertise, building upon their experience in the teaching of literacy. This would indeed be a positive development, provided that such teachers avoided the temptation of teaching these skills out of context, in the way that literacy skills have so often been taught. These cross-curricular skills do not *precede* the curriculum in any sense, but are taught *through* and *in* the curriculum. They should not and cannot be taught as part of a new-style remedial programme delivered outside the mainstream classroom.

Conclusion

We have suggested that the structure of the National Curriculum calls into question many of the traditional practices of special needs teachers. The existence of a common, commonly accessible curriculum weakens, and perhaps removes completely, the barriers between special needs and mainstream teaching. It requires, therefore, that special needs teachers carry out a thorough review of their current role. Many special needs teachers are already operating in a way that is not dissimilar to that outlined above; many others have a basis of skill and experience that can be adapted to meet the changing circumstances.

It is our view that the National Curriculum, for all its limitations and unfortunate political overtones, nonetheless offers an opportunity for a significant enhancement of the learning experiences offered to children with special needs. *Whether that opportunity will be grasped will in large part depend on the good-will, determination and, above all, imagination of special needs teachers.*

References

Bines, H. (1986) *Redefining Remedial Education.* Croom Helm, London.

Bines, H. (1988) 'Equality, community and individualism: the development and implementation of the "whole school approach" to special education needs' in Barton, L. (ed.) *The Politics of Special Educational Needs.* Falmer Press, London.

Department of Education and Science (1978) *Special Educational Needs* (The Warnock Report). HMSO, London.

Department of Education and Science and the Welsh Office (1987) *National Curriculum: Task Group on Assessment and Testing: A Report.*

Department of Education and Science and the Welsh Office (1987) *The National Curriculum 5 to 16: A Consultation Document.*

Gipps, C. and Gross, H. (1987) 'Children with special needs in the primary school: where are we now?', *Support for Learning,* 2, 43–8.

Gray, H. E. (ed.) (1988) *Management Consultancy in Schools.* Cassell, London.

Hart, S. (1986) 'In-class support teaching: tackling Fish', *British Journal of Special Education,* 13, 57–8.

National Curriculum Council (1989a) Circular No. 5. NCC, York.

National Curriculum Council (1989b) *English Key Stage 1: Non-Statutory Guidance.* NCC, York.

National Curriculum Council (1989c) *Science: Non-Statutory Guidance.* NCC, York.

Part IV
The Ocean of Literacy

22 The Family Reading Groups Movement

Cecilia Obrist and Anne Stuart

Introduction

Family reading groups have been established and developed for some years under a project supported by the Research Committee of the United Kingdom Reading Association (UKRA).

Family reading groups (FRGs) have been instituted for a number of reasons. They are intended to increase children's and parents' pleasure in books, to increase their knowledge of modern children's literature and to help awaken critical faculties in both children and adults. For many participating families, the FRG constitutes their first contact with their local library and librarian. As such, they have been considered an important step towards developing a reading habit. They have also been considered to be valuable in bringing children and parents into school in an informal way to follow a common interest with teachers and librarians.

Historical Review

In 1971 the UKRA Research Committee wanted to start research work at grassroots level and devised a short questionnaire asking the following three questions:

1 In your experience what are the main difficulties children have in learning to read?
2 What are the main difficulties you have found in teaching children to read?
3 In what areas in the teaching of reading would you welcome help and advice?

A pilot scheme was run in Bedfordshire using this questionnaire. The areas of highest concern were (a) lack of books in the home, and (b) lack of liaison between home and school.

At this time the South Bedfordshire Children's Book Group – a member of the Federation of Children's Book Groups – had become concerned to involve children more in its activities and had evolved a system of reading and reviewing books by children and parents.

The late Christina Wright, Young People's Librarian, and Cecilia Obrist were at that time involved both in UKRA and the Book Group. They decided to try reading and reviewing groups in schools. The first one was run as a pilot scheme in what was then a junior mixed and infants school in North Bedfordshire; it proved very successful. The headmaster Mr Prince also devised a written review sheet which was completed both by parents and children and which has been widely used since.

The number of FRGs nationwide is not known but there are well-established groups in many counties, and recently a number of school-based groups have been set up in the Greater Manchester area. Discussion in this chapter is based on published and unpublished evidence from these undertakings.

From the beginning FRGs organised by parents and FRGs organised by schools and libraries grew up side by side, variously involving parents, teachers, headteachers, and school and public librarians.

Each group develops its own style and tempo according to its composition, the ages of its children, the objectives of the professionals involved and the area served. All are characterised by enthusiastic professionals, regular meetings and discussions about books in an informal setting.

FRGs have most usually been started with a display of books from the schools' library service and a talk by a librarian or UKRA member on the value of literature. The children choose books to take home and either read alone or, if they are not able to read, for their parents to read to them. In about a month's time they all return and discuss the books.

Types of Family Reading Groups

There are *pre-school groups* run by parents in homes, play-schools or libraries; these take place in the afternoon. Books are provided by the schools' library service and are chosen mainly by parents from the central library with librarians advising.

Children start as young as two years old, or even less, and most of the children involved come initially through the play-schools. Nursery schools are also known to have very successful groups.

In some cases, reviews are written by the parents, who write down the reactions of the children. (Older children will write their own reviews.) From these reviews it is possible to see the books most enjoyed by the very young.

FRGs have also been run successfully in day nurseries by a multi-disciplinary team including social services, the public library and the psychological service. An interesting development was the help found for a few mothers who were unable to read.

Pre-school children who come to school with their parents may then become involved with FRG meetings. The FRG undoubtedly leads to early reading readiness by providing a context for shared reading and fostering reading for pleasure.

FRGs held in infant and lower schools generally meet for the last period of the afternoon. Parents come to the hall when they have collected their children from the classroom. FRGs with large numbers generally divide up into sub-groups of eight to ten parents and children who sit in circles to discuss the books among themselves.

Other schools have parents and children seated in semi-circles and each child talks about the book they have read. Then the parents also give their views. If the book has already been read by others in the FRG they may also give their opinion. Discussion of the particular book, or of others by the same author, may follow. Children may also sit more informally on mats on the floor with parents behind them on chairs.

Generally the person taking the meeting – the headteacher, a teacher, a librarian or one of a parents' committee formed to run the FRG – holds up the book for all to see. If it is illustrated the pages will be turned to show the illustrations. Frequently the child who has read the book will want to turn to a special illustration to reinforce what they are saying. The effect of talking about books and looking at illustrations is considerable. When the time to change books arrives the books that have been enthusiastically talked about are in great demand!

The discussion session is usually followed by a story told by the librarian or another person. Then there may be tea, squash and biscuits and everyone goes off to read in the home; very often children want to take out a book for a second or even a third time. The age groups chosen will depend entirely on the FRG. Schools generally consider carefully what age group to focus on in view of their own particular objectives. One primary school with a successful history of shared reading throughout the infant department wanted to emphasise to parents the importance of continuing to encourage reading for pleasure so they set up their group with lower juniors. The local public library has joined in and some meetings will be held in the library. It is hoped this will establish regular library use as these children move up to the junior department. Another school feels that an early start is vital and is basing its project on the reception class with younger siblings encouraged to join too. An infant school intending to phase out its published reading scheme is starting with the top infants and working down through the school. Two-form entry schools are advised not to invite everyone. This has been tried. Far too many people arriving for the initial meeting of an FRG, whether in school or library, is not the best way for a group to start off. If there were enough children in different age groups FRGs could operate on different days; however, this is liable to put too great a strain on the librarians. FRGs in schools can be run without staff participation but there is so much to be gained if a staff member can be present to join in the discussion.

Middle and upper school meetings generally take place in the evening, perhaps from 7 p.m. onwards so that working parents can attend. Fathers have been traditional story-tellers and they are likely to continue to enjoy this involvement with their children as much as mothers and older siblings do (Mann, 1971; McLean, 1985; Obrist, 1978; Thorpe, 1988). At the evening FRG meetings parents and children reading independently will both report back to the meeting.

The *book groups* which are members of the Federation of Children's Book Groups also run FRGs; these may take place in homes, libraries or schools. They follow the same pattern as the school meetings but are run by parents with a librarian who may be from either the schools' library service or the public library.

It has been found that regular dates for meetings, such as the first Wednesday in every month, are best. Some FRGs meet more frequently, and others only twice a term. However, once a month gives plenty of time to enjoy the books and yet is not too long a time that the books are forgotten.

Those who run FRGs must decide whether written reviews might be advantageous or whether they could stifle discussion, particularly if any parents are likely to have difficulty writing reviews. Nevertheless, it has been found that children are happy to write reviews. In some cases parents, and particularly fathers unable to attend meetings, will write comprehensive reviews; they are in this way able to make a useful and important contribution to the family aspect of the groups' functioning.

Effects of Family Reading Groups

1   FRGs increase the awareness of the range and what might be considered the best of modern children's literature. They can highlight the value of books which may otherwise be little known.

The discussion and reading of written reviews by parents and children on returning their books also gives librarians and teachers an insight into the reactions of the readers.

2   Parents and children find the contact with librarians and teachers much easier in the informal environment of the FRG. It has also been shown that teachers may well underestimate parents who, sometimes to their surprise, will come and take part.

The public librarians find that as their staff become known to parents and children the use of the public library increases; this may also occur where librarians from local libraries support a school FRG. This is valuable since several studies – Mann (1971), for example – have shown that a large proportion of the population do not go to public libraries after leaving school and have no confidence in their ability to use them either for reference or for reading for pleasure.

3   Pre-school children who attend FRGs learn how to handle books and become familiar with print. Sharing books and

discussing pictures promotes both language development and thinking. Incidentally and in a 'meaningful context', visual discrimination is heightened; attention, listening and speaking are developed and 'taking turns' can be easily modelled and naturally followed.

4   Headteachers and parents have found that reading ability is increased as a result of greater interest in books and the greater incentive to read although there has been no widespread and systematic research on this aspect of FRGs (see also the Bradford Book Flood Project (Ingham, 1982) and Hunter (1982–4)).

5   Teachers and parents become aware of children's interests and problems. In discussing situations that occur in books they can express their point of view which may highlight something that is worrying them in real life or that they do not understand. Parents in giving their opinions on situations arising in stories can make clear what they consider acceptable behaviour. One headmaster has expressed the view that the discussion of values and ethics arising in this way is of great importance.

6   Parents, teachers and children enjoy looking at the display of books provided by the libraries and choosing at leisure and with discussion. Children enthuse other children to read books they have enjoyed.

Important Characteristics of Family Reading Groups

The particular strengths of FRGs which foster such results are parental involvement, their voluntary nature and the informal group discussions.

It is now widely agreed that informed parental interest and participation is a significant factor in the development of positive attitudes to reading (Tizard et al., 1981; Ingham, 1982; Topping and Wolfendale, 1981) and a number of schemes to involve parents in the early stages of learning to read have been published (Waterland, 1985; Branston and Provis, 1986; Morgan, 1986). Children who go to libraries with their parents from an early age are more likely to grow up regarding reading as an enjoyable activity: Nigel Hall (1984) emphasises the importance of pre-school experience which teaches the knowledge and purpose of literacy. Parental support, however, should not be confined to the early stages of enjoying books and reading. Children need the continued encouragement and genuine interest of adults, particularly their parents, if they are to become readers for life.

The unforced nature of the enterprise is important. Members grow in confidence largely because they have control over the extent to which they join in discussion, which books they read and indeed whether they attend or not. Books provided are not reading primers or the set books of the secondary literature syllabus, nor are they even junior 'classics'. Books are very often chosen because other children have recommended them. At FRG meetings younger children decide for themselves whether they will read a book, share it with a member of the family, or listen to the story being read. Parents report much more relaxed and enjoyable reading with their children when the story itself, rather than the child's reading performance, is the issue. Enjoyment of books is a prime factor in motivating a child to read (Prentice, 1987). The value of using 'real' books rather than reading schemes has been advanced by Waterland (1985). We would want to add that developing a reading habit may not depend so much on the selectivity or format of this structural reading material but on the content of the stories themselves. That may be the crucial variable, along with the teacher's presentation and considering the children's views on what are good stories in whatever packaging.

In the informal group discussions, whether based in libraries or schools, all parties find it easy to relate to one another, and barriers, real or imaginary, are broken down. Parents attending an FRG for reception children said they had learned how to use a story book more profitably by observing the class teacher's interactions with children. Where teachers and librarians work together each benefits from the other's particular professional knowledge and skills. Confidence grows in an atmosphere of interest and respect where each member's opinion is attended to by the rest of the group, both children and adults.

The special collection of books is displayed face up on tables or even on the floor. This seems to help children to choose more easily, no doubt because it is less daunting than the full library stock displayed spineways on shelves, but also because it has been carefully selected and then promoted by both members and professionals in discussion.

Virtually all FRGs rely heavily on the schools' library service for their supply of books and for the expertise of the librarian. (Librarians from the public library also participate in some areas but more often than not staffing levels are insufficient for this.) Unfortunately the proposed changes in funding are putting this service under serious threat, particularly as the schools' library service is not mandatory. Already some recently organised FRGs have been told that future loans of books including some bi-lingual stock are not guaranteed.

Family Reading Groups and the National Curriculum

Readers familiar with the English attainment targets proposed by Cox (DES, 1988) and in the Orders and programmes published to date (Key Stage 1, 1989) will already appreciate the ways in which FRGs can help.

Parental involvement is recommended. 'Parents should share books with their children from their earliest days, read aloud to them and talk about the stories they have read together' (Cox, 1988, para. 2.3); 'It is recognised that enjoyment is important: children read best when they are enjoying themselves' (para. 9.3).

Discussions at FRGs would seem ideal media for certain speaking and listening targets: a progression from participating 'as speakers and listeners in group activities' (Revised Attainment Target (RAT) Level 1.i) to the ability to 'speak freely to a larger audience of peers and adults' and 'the ability to debate constructively, advocating and justifying a point of view' (Level 5).

In FRG meetings children are communicating not in a contrived situation but to an interested, informed and sometimes critical audience. Furthermore the topic of discussion – books read and enjoyed – coincides with reading targets: these suggest that children should 'begin to talk about the content of stories' (RAT Level 1.iv); 'describe what has happened in a story' (RAT Level 2.iv) and show an ability to 'recall significant details and to talk about setting, plot and characters' (RAT Level 3.iii). Later levels require children to express opinions 'providing supporting evidence from the text' (Level 4) and later still they should 'read regularly and voluntarily over a still wider range of prose and verse' and 'show developing tastes and preferences over an increased range of materials' (Level 5).

Conclusion

A major strength of FRGs is their flexibility. FRGs should not follow a prescribed format and each FRG can develop its own structure based on the needs of its members.

FRGs have now been established for some years. The results indicate how these groups, if supported and encouraged, can do much to develop the reading interests of the young and establish reading as a lifelong pursuit.

Acknowledgement

The UKRA Research Committee acknowledges with appreciation the recently awarded grant from the DES to carry out a two-year study of FRGs. At the time of writing the project was in its early stages. We look forward to providing results of the exploratory and evaluative study in due course.

References

Branston, P. and Provis, M. (1986) *Children and Parents Enjoying Reading.* Hodder and Stoughton, London.

Department of Education and Science (1988) *English for Ages 5 to 11* (The Cox Report). HMSO, London.

Department of Education and Science (1989) *English in the National Curriculum, Key Stage 1.* HMSO, London.

Hall, N. (1984) 'Conveying the message that reading is necessary, valuable and pleasant', in Dennis, D. (ed.) *Reading: Meeting Children's Special Needs.* Heinemann, London.

Hunter, C. M. (1982–4) *Talking with Books.* Interim Report and Final Reports, Occasional Publication, University of Leicester, School of Education.

Ingham, J. (1982) *Books and Reading Development.* Heinemann, London.

Mann, P. (1971) *Books: Buyers and Borrowers.* Andre Deutsch, London.

McClean, J. (1985) 'A study of voluntary reading across the Secondary age range and the role of Groups formed in two Secondary schools to extend and support pupils' voluntary reading'. M.A. diss., Institute of Education, London.

Morgan, R. (1986) *Helping Children Reading: The Paired Reading Approach*. Methuen, London.

Obrist, C. (1978) *How to Run Family Reading Groups*. Occasional Publication, United Kingdom Reading Association, Ormskirk.

Prentice, J. (1987) 'Real books and paired reading in context', *Reading*, 21, 159–68.

Thorpe, D. (1988) *Reading for Fun*. Cranfield Press, Cranfield.

Tizard, B., Mortimore, J. and Burchell, B. (1981) *Involving Parents in Nursery and Infant Schools*. Grant McIntyre, London.

Topping, K. and Wolfendale, S. (eds) (1985) *Parental Involvement in Children's Reading*. Croom Helm, London.

Waterland, L. (1985) *Read with me: An Apprenticeship Approach to Reading*. Thimble Press, Stroud.

23 UKRA Members' Responses to Recent Reports

Sue Beverton and Morag Hunter-Carsch

Background

This chapter provides a brief depiction of the responses of UKRA members to a range of government reports that have led up to and include the creation of the National Curriculum. The chapter illustrates some ways in which the members who work in the education system in various capacities, mostly in close contact with children, have taken on the task of engaging with, understanding and commenting upon the issues raised in and through the various government reports.

This review of the membership's responses is derived directly from members' comments at every stage of the consultative process in which they actively engaged. Responses were made as a result of an open invitation circulated in the UKRA newsletter, and in letters to every local council secretary and to every area convener in the UK. The forms of response varied, including telephoned messages as well as written responses and submissions which contained not only members' reactions but samples of children's work.

The mass of data which represents the range of responses to the various reports constitutes a challenge to represent in a brief and coherent manner. At every stage of the process, all contributions were taken into account, all views and opinions reported, where possible fully. For the purpose of this chapter, it is essential to condense very considerably. We have therefore analysed responses to three sets of documents. The first set includes the report of the Task Group on Assessment and Testing (TGAT) and a prior review internal to UKRA (a survey of members' views on professional development, UKRA's role and teacher education carried out between 1984 and 1986). Results of the UKRA survey are examined for major themes. These are taken as a 'base-line' independent of the recent government reports. The members' views are then related to their response to the TGAT Report (December 1987). These two clusters of responses are linked since they both occurred chronologically prior to the reports directly concerning content of the curriculum.

The second set of responses deals with the Kingman Report (DES, 1988a).

The third set consists of responses to the first Cox Report (DES, 1988b), the NCC Consultative Report (1989) and the *Non-Statutory Guidelines for English Key Stage 1* (NCC, 1989).

Emergent Themes in Members' Responses

The reader will realise that the three sets of responses are not necessarily tapping the views of the same individuals although there is the characteristic tendency of those who are most active professionally to take part in any opportunity such as was afforded them by the consultative nature of the Government's approach to the design and development of the National Curriculum and the Association's invitation to members to make a shared as well as individual response where they wished to do so. The Association has taken care to offer members every opportunity to respond. The extent of follow-up of all the local councils of UKRA and the use of regional and annual conferences for consultative discussions suggest that this aim has been achieved in that each of the sets of responses appears to include responses from a range of education-related professionals and others, thus representing the diverse nature of the UKRA membership.

It transpires that the same major themes or areas of concern recur and are developed in a striking manner in the progression of responses. It is to be hoped that the implications of these emergent themes will be recognised by educational leaders and decision-makers since the themes represent professionally voiced, shared concerns. They are remarkable in their consistency. The themes are:

1   assessment which is systematic and regular is valuable provided it is clearly related to learning purpose and aims and provides feedback for the learner;

2 a sense of tension between national and local implications
   regarding what teachers can realistically undertake with regard
   to assessment and curriculum delivery;
3 the need for in-service education for teachers (Inset) and classroom support which is relevant and appropriate.

The following discussion considers these three strands of concern
as they emerge from within the context of each set of responses.

1 TGAT and Before

The UKRA survey on professional development revealed four
broad areas of interest: teachers' theoretical knowledge, application
of methodology, pupil assessment, and resources.

The kinds of theoretical knowledge respondents felt they needed
included knowledge about various aspects of the reading process
and the ability to recognise the implications of this for whole
language development and total development of the child. Matters
such as what contribution linguistics can make to the teacher's
professional expertise regarding language development were raised,
as was the need to acquire skills to identify the nature and extent
of individual differences in learning.

Skill in the use of a range of methodologies was frequently
cited as necessary, together with the ability to select and evaluate
methods appropriately. Although these points were made largely
in connection with the reading process, their more generalised
relevance across the curriculum was regularly mentioned. Respondents warned against over-reliance upon any one methodology and
noted that teachers play an important role in generating pupil
motivation and enthusiasm; also that pupils need time (their own
time in school) in which to read.

Assessment was posed as a problem area, especially for beginner
teachers who were very likely to be unaware of the vast range of
factors that need to be taken into account. Respondents appreciated
well   the   need   for   record   keeping,   especially   for   the
primary–secondary transition and other transfer purposes, and to
recognise when something is going wrong. It was also seen to be
desirable for teachers to be able to put right any difficulties once
they had been identified.

Resourcing the classroom well enough for the teacher to do his/
her job properly appeared frequently as a major issue. Needs

included wider ranges of printed materials for children; teachers to acquaint themselves with manuals for published schemes; and back-up materials and facilities (including time) for teachers to develop, modify or discard resources.

The report on the survey stresses that throughout these four areas, but especially with regard to resources, much more emphasis needs to be placed on 'In-service education of a kind that takes into account teachers' felt needs'. The reader will be able to relate these few areas to our three recurrent concerns of assessment, local and national tension and resourcing.

Turning to the UKRA response to the TGAT Report, the theme of assessment is uppermost in the respondents' minds, given the brief of the Task Group. Indeed, we might even expect to find no mention of other concerns. In fact, the Association's response both deals in detail with the full report and makes strong points about Inset provision, resourcing and local and national issues.

In summary, the Association's response starts by supporting the constructive attitude of the TGAT Report and agreeing with the perspective set out early in the Report's introduction (paras 1–6). This perspective places assessment at the heart of children's learning and establishes it as serving the curriculum. The Report concludes with forty-four recommendations and it is to each of these that the response is directed. Substantial areas of agreement are apparent, for example, over the need for formative and summative assessment and for profiling in principle.

Interestingly, however, there is a strong note of dissent from Recommendaton 3, that it should not be possible to separate out individual performances on assessment. The Association feels this does not accord with the Report's ethos of the aims of formative assessment. Underlying this could there be a concern that nationally a decision may be taken which would remove information relevant to teachers' work?

More subtle, perhaps, is the dissent from Recommendation 4 where the Report advises that pupil attitudes should not come into formal assessment. The response points out that attitude is crucial in learning, and that information on attitude could usefully inform the move from assessment to planning.

Concern that the governing factor in the style of collection of national assessment data might be 'convenience' sharpened the response to the Report's relevant proposals. Indeed, the suggested streamlined format in the Report raised anxieties that recurred throughout the response in various forms, wherever the principle of securing the effective functioning of all schools was felt to be at risk.

The response is also at pains to express its concerns about the time and resources needed for in-service training. It points out that teacher-training programmes would be required to cover a wide range of elements in an assessment system that attempted to be systematic, to be objectives-based and to combine national norms and local moderation procedures.

The reader will appreciate that both the Report and the UKRA response covered many more items than have been discussed here. The aim has been to give the flavour of the response rather than its full detail. The reader will have recognised that again the three strands of concern identified at the outset are amply reinforced in the response.

2 The Kingman Era

As a general observation the Kingman Report marks a watershed in attitude among the teaching force of the membership; beforehand, without anything substantive in a curricular sense in front of them, many members tended to be wary of the ability of a government-appointed body to table constructive, sensible and appropriate ideas for curricular reform. Yet a close reading of the Report itself revealed less cause for apprehension, particularly when it was remembered this was but a small part of the whole business of the teaching of English. And just a few months later, when the Association's response to the Cox Committee was reported, the membership's tendency to wariness had given way to positive thinking, in which the challenge had definitely been taken up and the emphases moved towards problems of illiteracy, poor communication and multi-lingual needs.

How had this seeming volte-face happened? The answer may lie in two sources – (1) the immediately preceding history of events and (2) teachers' need for practical proposals.

So – to go back to the time of the beginning of this 'transformation', the body of the Association's 'further evidence'. Submission to the Kingman Committee (August 1987) presents its initial section under the heading 'Conceptual Confusion' – almost a cry of warning. This section was written in the wake of having made a condensed initial submission followed by oral evidence, by invitation of the Committee and further written evidence on request of the Committee.

It highlights the fact that the Committee did indeed face much conceptual confusion existing at large, over such notions as 'correct grammar', the place of literature in the curriculum, the relationship between what teachers need to know and what children need to know, theory and practice, what and how to teach, and description or prescription. Elsewhere the submission notes, with some insistence, that clarification is needed on, amongst other issues, how to maintain and transfer the Bullock Report's holistic emphasis on language across the curriculum to the curricular specialism focus of the English 5–16 paper.

In the submission's summary, six main points are made. All of these can readily be subsumed under the headings of the earlier identified three strands of the Association's concern. The need for *purposeful* assessment is clearly present in Summary Point 5, which stresses that 'particular attention is required for methods of recording progress and problems on a long-term basis in order to provide most appropriately for the range of individual needs' and that 'the work of the APU [Assessment Performance Unit] is pertinent and the dissemination of their findings in *contexts which permit ready feedback and on-going dialogue* is essential' (editors' italics).

The awareness of tension between national and local level over what is realistic and the need for relevant and appropriate Inset and classroom support was omnipresent in both the original and further submissions of evidence. Just one example will suffice:

Teachers do need to have more information about how to describe how the English language functions and to engage in professional discussion . . . *but the way in which such information and understanding is achieved is crucial to the success of its implementation* . . . not as 'instruction' to pupils but as involvement in problem-solving . . . exploring the richness of language and communication. (editors' italics)

After the Kingman Report had been read and digested, members of UKRA reported acceptance that the Committee had basically come up with some sympathetic and usable ideas. There were still reservations, however, being expressed about the same strands of concern. Some sensed that a political drive behind the Kingman Report might be outweighing educational priorities.

Teachers are put under stress by this worry over standards.

We feel there is a dichotomy between Kingman recommendations and testing proposed under the National Curriculum. Where does that leave us?

Kingman is aimed at teachers' performance rather than pupil performance, which leads to the problem of accountability and possibly payment by results.

There is a sense that Kingman might be implemented due to Government pressure.

Will assessment make teaching more formal and make us move away from the more individual teaching we prefer to implement?

Others found themselves embroiled in arguments over interpreting what exactly Kingman was trying to say or not to say. One discussion group reported:

We had a heated discussion over teaching grammar. There is great anxiety here, despite what Kingman has to say. Some of us insisted you teach English through what children have written and said, and that parts of speech are not necessary to know. Others argued that the 'Basics of English' have to be taught, that children are reading less and less and the higher or further on through education pupils go, the more they fall backwards. One member who happily teaches English through literature, does not see himself as servicing the rest of the school, correcting faults. We had a big row and the meeting broke up in confusion.

All the above extracts are from reports from discussion groups who met at a Northern Regional UKRA Special Conference on 11 June 1988 to discuss the implications of the Kingman Report. These views of over 200 members, together with the proceedings from a simultaneous conference in the South, were submitted along with responses from every English, Welsh and Scottish Area of the Association for consideration by a small working party of UKRA's National Executive.

The outcome constituted UKRA's response to the Kingman Report. It is perhaps hardly surprising that this response carried forward with it the same areas of concern as originally expressed by individual members. What may be surprising is the extent of the emphasis evident on the three emergent areas of concern in what effectively involved a much wider representation to this response than previously to the TGAT Report. One extract may suffice to exemplify the beginning of the turn-around, from a somewhat apprehensive and critical attitude to one or more positively and energetically constructive contribution to the next stage of the dialogue: '12. We endorse the importance of noting the relationship between comprehension and expression. This should be discussed and developed in subsequent work.' Cross-reference is then made to a previous similar point in the response to the Report. The document continues: '13. We are pleased to see the acknowledgement of the specificity of tasks used for assessment purposes and the warnings about the possible "backwash effects of testing" as a danger of limited understanding or misunderstanding of the recommendations of the TGAT Report and the Attainment Targets.'

It may perhaps be suggested that the very nature of the professional encouragement being offered by the Association to its members to engage directly in the dialogue and development was having an effect on the individual members' feelings about their own worth and relevance to the wider development in education.

3 Cox and Beyond

As the core curriculum areas were developed, UKRA's responses to the Science and Mathematic working parties' reports were collated by a working party from the UKRA National Executive Committee, assisted by a group of teacher-members. The NEC Working Party responded to the invitation from the DES to make comment to the Cox Committee, a working group on English, on attainment targets at ages 7 and 11. The UKRA submission concentrated on the following issues:

1   the need to state targets in terms that permit contextualised assessment;
2   ensuring a process-orientation to the concept of learning;
3   devising records which show what is typical, optimal and weak in pupils' work; and
4   taking account of text features that we already know to be important and features which as yet we know relatively little about but more knowledge of which could enhance learning.

There is some difference of focus between the content of the above submission to the Cox working group and the following series of comments from UKRA members on the ensuing Cox Report. The comments were amongst those submitted by members who responded to the UKRA newsletter request to comment on the Report or who responded to local council or Area Conveners' encouragement. The following responses are represented in two parts: (1) an account from one local council and (2) examples of views drawn from different areas of the UK.

The Main Points from the Responses to the First Cox Report by One UKRA Local Council

1 General Reactions

The first Cox Report was greeted by

a generally favourable response . . . however . . . the report failed to consider how children learn although considerable relief was expressed that it was not '*prescriptive as expected*'.

Practical suggestions are now needed for its implementation in the classroom.

2 Points of Agreement

The implementation of the document will raise awareness.

The document's respect for teacher judgement is welcomed as there must be weight given to the writing process as well as the product.

3 Points of Disagreement

Speaking and Listening

There should be differentiation between productive speaking and receptive listening which would be parallel to the differentiation between reading and writing (links to these needed).

Children with unclear speech but no impediment are not covered.

At Level 5 why has narrative been dropped?

Reading 1

Level 1. Lacks a profile of emergent reading . . . too general a description.

Level 2. Readers always use more than one strategy.

Reading 2

There is little awareness that non-fiction books may display very different text forms.

Level 1. The separation between fiction and non-fiction is at times artificial.

Levels 1–4. There could be some indication that non-fiction books can be enjoyable as well as have an instrumental purpose.

The Report uses terms which tend to imply that teachers have considerable awareness of linguistic patterning, e.g. 'Semantic and syntactic awareness'.

Writing

There is some suggestion that writing is not inter-active. How are liveliness and imagination to be rated?

Some matters come rather late, e.g. non-chronological writing.

There is no note of appropriateness of vocabulary.

Spelling

Too big a jump between Levels 1 and 2.

Inventive spelling is a difficult concept for some teachers to cope with.

Handwriting

Level 3. Cursive writing should appear earlier.

4 *Other Comments*

To what extent are 'best samples' unaided?

How is the recorded assessment to show that some children may fall between levels or operate at different levels?

Other local councils of UKRA also found much to comment upon in the Cox Report. There was a generally positive attitude in the responses. For example:

We applaud the rationale/philosophy/stance taken on defining the reading process. We applaud the acknowledgement of the importance of spelling and handwriting. We applaud the clear delineation between ability and current language attainment.

It was pleasing to see that the work of the National Writing Project was used to frame the attainment targets in writing.

Pleased to note the emphasis on oracy and drama and the inclusion of media studies and information technology.

Nevertheless, the old familiar strands of concern were still much in evidence. Thus frequently occurring comments included the following:

Teachers will need to be trained in assessment and testing.

Worry that assessments will be time-consuming – how will a teacher find the time to observe the child?

Will there be a danger of 'teaching for testing'?

Yet there is amongst the responses evidence of a further stage of development in the membership's view of what is happening to their profession and to education in general. The members appear to be broadening their ideas and interests. It is as if the fact that Cox is making firm proposals and beds itself firmly within current good practice is encouraging teachers to think more positively, constructively and critically. But the criticisms are no longer so defensive. Some broader, new concerns were prominent:

Bilingual children are at a disadvantage, especially at age 7. Could some credit not be given for their fluency in their mother tongue?

The National Curriculum will have a profound effect upon children with Special Needs. Will streaming be necessary?

Critical comments included the following:

If resources had been provided for implementing the Bullock Report there would have been no need for the Cox Report.

The confusion about Standard English (here referred to as primarily a written form) is shown by previous statements which align it with Spoken English. The whole argument seems unresolved.

In the period of time since the first Cox Report up to writing this chapter, more official documents have appeared in this field. These include the National Curriculum Council's Consultation Document on English Curriculum, the Government's Draft Proposals, NCC's proposals for English for ages 5 to 16, the *Non-Statutory Guidelines for English Key Stage 1* and the second Cox

Report. Four further documents now exist since responses to the first Cox Report were first formulated. All those documents have served to endorse many of the principles that Cox put forward. As each successive document arrived consultation time was ever shorter. This is unfortunate since the whole business has accelerated away from the possibility of interaction with teachers at the grassroots level. At the same time, however, teachers seem to feel happier with the bringing into existence of a clearer framework within which they can consider how best to operate. They have greater certainties than ever before as to what is expected from them and their pupils.

Many dangers may be lurking in the new waters. Teachers may find themselves 'teaching for testing', as one respondent had put it. And what about the trialling and further development of the National Curriculum? How will it look in 10 to 20 years' time? If the kind of professional participation in the consultation process that we have been involved in were to become a thing of the past, it would be a pity. One of the underlying aims of this chapter has been to show that given the opportunity, professional bodies are responsibly ready to contribute at every stage of the consultative process and that through their forum for growth through debate the education system can be enriched, leading more effectively to the implementation of relevant well-considered changes.

24 Celebrating Literacy

Morag Hunter-Carsch

International Literacy Year

1990 is proclaimed as International Literacy Year (ILY) by Unesco. The aim in observing ILY is 'to contribute to greater understanding by world public opinion of the various aspects of the problem of illiteracy and to intensified efforts to spread literacy and education' (Unesco, 1988). The assumption is that 'eradication of illiteracy is inseparable from the objective of primary education for all' and that achieving literacy is part of 'the struggle for development, justice, greater equality, respect of cultures and recognition of the human dignity of all and the claims of each to an economic, social and political role in society and the fruits which derive therefrom'. Unesco further considers it should be a priority objective of the international community as a whole and of Unesco to eradicate illiteracy by the year 2000 (Unesco, 1988).

Literacy, Human Rights and the National Curriculum

If one accepts the above view of the potential and moral imperative of literacy, it becomes apparent that the teaching of literacy must be guided by such principles from the outset. The Concise Oxford Dictionary's (5th ed.) definition of literacy which is simply 'ability to read and write' then needs to be translated into the kinds of guidelines for teachers which are currently being developed on the basis of the National Curriculum in England for ages 5 to 16.

Even a cursory glance at the June 1989 proposals for the National Curriculum in England indicates the need to understand (1) the relationship of reading and writing to listening and speaking and (2) the relationship of teaching to learning in the process of developing literacy and thus of 'eradicating illiteracy'. Indeed the idea of eradicating illiteracy is perhaps an unfortunate one since the very nature of literacy involves building on the existing human facility for communicating through spoken language and the myriad patterns of non-verbal communication which support culturally developed patterns of interaction. This is particularly pertinent as we move into an era in which information technology has advanced to such a point that much of what used to be handwritten or possibly typewritten communication now takes the form of computer print-out and can be fax-transmitted with the potential for simultaneous, automatic audio-visual 'translation' (see Chapter 18 'Lit-oracy, a Technical Breakthrough', pp. 160–7).

The idea of literacy which employs such notions of 'writing' is somewhat different from the kind of encoding which requires careful formulation of individual letters or symbols which represent meanings in either ideographic or phonemic patterning. The idea of writing in terms of calligraphy, an art form, particularly with its associations with poetry and the visio-spatial factors including shape of the message, then needs to be related to the craft, design and technological features as well as the audio-temporal factors including rhythm involved in the arts of music, dance and drama. All of these ideas are implicit in the foundation curricular subject specialisation and require to be related also to the content (the actual messages and meaning) being taught or learned through the other core subjects, mathematics and science as well as the foundation subjects.

Achieving Functional Literacy

The question then arises as to whether primary education, as we know it and as it is being developed through the National Curriculum in England and Wales, can provide a framework within which there can be developed in young children the kind of interest in listening and speaking as well as reading and writing which predisposes them to want to communicate and to go on communicating with their peers across language and cultural differences as well as within the national and local context which includes linguistic and cultural diversity.

There is also the related question of how to assess functional literacy in adults as well as children since the previously held rough measures employed the concept of reading age. A person having a reading age of 7 years was suggested as being 'semi-literate', and a reading age of 9 years indicated 'basic literacy'. The measured reading comprehension difficulty of some popular daily newspapers was in those terms rated around a reading age of 9 years and derived from readability assessment procedures, many of which concerned recognition and length of single words and of sentences rather than understanding of meaning or, more particularly, of levels of meaning. So much more is now known about the reading process and text construction and analysis that reading difficulty should be more broadly considered in terms of the range of factors that are pertinent to the process, not selectively by the criteria of word or sentence length. Reading ability should likewise be considered in terms of a wide range of factors and perhaps, most particularly, in terms of specific purposes.

It is in that sense that we would wish to return to the idea of functional literacy, to reconsider whether a primary education should and can equip everyone to be functionally literate, or whether it can realistically offer only conditions in which children can learn how to read and write sufficiently effectively to meet their 'needs'. Inevitably we come back to the question of the value judgements associated with any assumption about needs, particularly when they are described and indeed prescribed in terms other than those defined by the individual.

It is important in this connection to distinguish between (a) individual needs that are inborn (e.g. for food and air), (b) social needs which arise out of the sociation patterns on which individual survival depends (e.g. the division of labour and the regulation of patterns of affective expression) and (c) conditioned or pro-grammed 'wants' (e.g. patterns of self-preservation and consumption).

The Scope of Primary English in the National Curriculum for Fostering World Literacy

The key to developing literacy would thus seem to include knowing the purposes for which literacy is helpful. Amongst these is the recognition that the written or printed word differs from the spoken word in the availability for its consideration, without the requirement to memorise it. Thus the printed message not only contains the content meaning, but provides an *aide-memoir* for the listener or reader.

It also permits examination and re-examination, and can be checked, analysed, evaluated, enjoyed or rejected. It is thus not only a way of receiving and giving messages but of remembering and developing thinking. It is not simply a tool for action, for information processing or communication but an aid to reflection. This is part of its power. The challenge that this constitutes for the educator involves the relating of the means of becoming literate to the ends or purposes of literacy – a challenge similar in its significance to assisting children to understand and appreciate both freedom and responsibility. The distinction may need to be made between responsible use of (a) the freedom to read and write and mastery of the symbol system and (b) conventions of written language. In this context the development of reflective readers and writers includes media education.

The National Curriculum in English provides plenty of scope for such development. From the beginning of formal schooling at 5 years the emphasis is on reading and writing for meaning, writing for different purposes and audiences, and reading so as to 'understand and respond to all types of writing, as well as to develop information-retrieval strategies for the purpose of study'. Even within the first key stage, Levels 1–3 for ages 5 to 7 years, there is the expectation that pupils should be able to 'appreciate meanings beyond the literal' (Attainment Target (AT) 2, Level 3.iv) and 'devise a clear set of questions that will enable them to select and use appropriate information sources and reference books from the class and school library' (AT 2, Level 3.v). They should also at Level 3 be able to 'begin to revise and redraft . . . paying attention to meaning and clarity' in writing (AT 3, Level 3.v). Teachers are encouraged to engage children in media education which 'seeks to increase children's critical understanding of the media . . . and to develop systematically children's critical and creative powers through analysis and production of media artefacts' (9.6). There is also the appreciation of the substantial pool of linguistic competence which exists amongst bilingual children and the clear statement that 'one of the main aims of the National Curriculum is a knowledge of other languages for all pupils' (10.4). The importance of providing literature which is drawn from different countries is endorsed as a way of 'introducing children to ideas and feelings of cultures different from their own' (7.5).

The following ideas constitute some practical ways of fostering world literacy. They are also directly related to developing Primary English in the National Curriculum. It is hoped that readers of this book will feel free to try out any of the suggestions and may be willing to share examples of their work encouraging children towards the achievement of this worthy aim of International Literacy Year and the decade of the 1990s, in which it is hoped that literacy can be achieved internationally. An invitation form is included at the end of this chapter. Any enquiries, results of projects, examples of work or reports sent to UKRA will be acknowledged by UKRA. Materials arriving prior to UKRA's 27th Annual Conference (July 1990) may form part of the workshop materials on the topic of International Literacy Year. Subject to contributors' permission they may also be listed and shared as part of a report on UKRA's contribution to ILY. We hope you will enjoy contributing in some way to both ILY and the decade of the '90s work in this field, and that you will join with us not only in developing, but in celebrating, literacy.

Reference

Unesco (1988) *Adult Education Information Notes*, Special no. 4.

Notes for the Class Teacher: Communicating with Children from another Country

Idea 1. Making an Audiotaped Message

Introduction

This idea is developed on the basis of Phil Pinnington's (Ariel Trust) approach to making a radio programme, as introduced to delegates at the 26th Annual Conference of UKRA at Ormskirk in July 1989.

For information on a link address contact to schools or teachers overseas, please complete the form appended to this chapter. There is already in existence an established network of European, Australian, Asian and other International Reading Association Affiliates. Recent requests, particularly for practical, school-based links, have been received from Japan and Hong Kong.

To identify links with all areas of listening, speaking, reading and writing attainment targets and guidelines for programmes of study in the National Curriculum for English and for developing communication across the curriculum, please consult all the National Curriculum guidelines. With a real audience in mind, and a need to get to know that audience, it will quickly become evident how easily connections are made across core and foundation subject attainment targets, particularly in linking language and technological aspects of the curriculum.

Preparation

Decide on the country for your ILY link and discuss what you already know about the life of school children of the same age in that country and how they learn to read and write. List questions, particularly about their language(s) if it is not English. You may wish to show videotapes of children learning in schools in other countries such as Finland and Sweden to prompt discussion of similarities and differences (e.g. Thames Television's 'Seeing and Doing' programmes, Spring 1988). Then you may wish to extend the discussion to consider the country of your choice, possibly a Third World country.

Plan a very simple introductory audiotaped programme for children of the same age in that country, aiming to say who the speakers are, why they are making the tape and what they would like to say, and to ask about learning reading and writing in that country.

Action

1 Using a cassette tape recorder **encourage all the children to speak** into the recorder saying in turn, 'Hello, my name is . . . . I am . . . years old'. This is usually speedy, easy and enjoyable to replay immediately. The variety of voices, and interest in hearing their own, usually builds confidence and can readily be 'improved' or lengthened after a practice run by adding a short comment to the name and age; for example on a favourite pastime, a pet, a book or a television programme.

2 The problem might be to get the individual youngsters to be brief and to stick to the agreed topic so a chance might be given then to **make notes** of a given number of words (e.g. 20 words) and then in turn to **read their notes**. This can seem quite professional – like writing or editing a script as part of work in media education (*English for ages 5 to 16*, June 1989, para. 9.6). The notes should be kept for later use in compiling a written 'transcript' or commentary.

3 These introductory remarks indicate who the speakers are and provide a little sense of their personalities and interests. The next step is to prepare a statement on what the children want to share and tell their audience about the way they learn to read and write and what they want to ask about how their audience learns. Given a fairly tight structure of steps (e.g. (a) what to tell and (b) what to ask) and a limited time (possibly 2–5 minutes) even quite young children of six or seven years can often **work in pairs or small groups to plan what kinds of things to ask and to share**.

They can then check, with the teacher's help where relevant, what the range of questions and comments should include. Overlaps can be acknowledged, appreciated and **a sample, if not all, of the questions and comments can be recorded**. The children's interest and the momentum of the programme can be maintained if the second step is dealt with fairly speedily by the teacher. If the groups of children are very much engaged in discussion and planning and are enjoying their work on preparing exactly what to say or ask, it can be worthwhile to extend the planning time and to prepare a series of very short recordings of different groups' contributions. Each group should appoint a speaker, if not everyone wants to contribute spontaneously. Usually there is considerable interest, attention and, of course, silence, as individuals make their recordings. **'Turn-taking' is encouraged** and a critical, evaluative stance may be adopted by the children as well as a supportive and encouraging one by those who are listeners in the exchange while planning and recording. After two or three contributors have been recorded it can be very helpful to replay and thus give an opportunity for the children's own reactions to their work to be shared.

4 Before sending the audiotape to its destination, it may be necessary to check that the receiving school has a cassette recorder and batteries or an electrically compatible energy source. If contact is being made with a school with very limited technological resources, it may be necessary to arrange for a fund drive to provide the 'ILY link school' with a tape recorder, cassette and batteries for this particular project to be successful in achieving its first objective, 'to communicate'. Although the exercise in making an introductory audiotape can be valuable in itself, it is so much more exciting for all the contributors to be able to hear a return audiotape on which children reciprocate in another language the names and patterns of which can quickly become a source of real linguistic as well as cultural interest. The interest in continuing the communication is the more easily fostered.

Idea 2. Making a Book

The following ideas are broadly inspired by the 'Talking with Books Project' which involved children in a multi-ethnic inner-city school in Leicester. The project revealed the close relationship between developing interest in reading and writing and the development of literacy. Both were found to be closely related with the development of speaking and listening and hearing oneself think in the process of reading and writing for meaning. The handling of books, and familiarising with the range of forms which story takes, were matters in which children gained confidence through the use of both their home languages and English.

As a follow-up to the above idea of making an audiotape, or for its own worth, it is fairly easy to encourage children to work in pairs, groups or as a class to make a book. Using the audiotape material as a starter, for example, they might want to make an illustrated transcript. The illustrations would likely include **portraits** of themselves. The discussion which could be developed as an integral part of the planning and preparation of the descriptions in words, perhaps of several languages, as well as critical planning of **design, art and craft**, possibly **computer technology** and likely employment of **reference skills**.

If making a book is undertaken independently of the audiotape idea, it may still be useful to employ audiotaping at the stages of planning, 'telling' the story or re-reading it aloud to identify pieces which may need **redrafting**.

The topics on which interesting books can be made for children of a similar age in another land are extensive. Apart from writing and illustrating imaginative stories, there can be much pleasure and constructive language and literacy development involved in collecting and producing a **book of songs, poems and prayers**. The children like to **write new songs, poems or prayers**, or to **write those with which they are familiar**. The inclusion of **musical notation, photographs** and the range of illustrations which they may think of are all likely to provide interesting material and will undoubtedly involve them in constructive discussion. Planning for such paired or group work may need to include the allocation not only of time for on-going project work, but the space or place in which to continue it. (See also 'writing table' and other ideas shared by Michael and Jackson in *Responding to Children's Writing*, SCOLA/COPE, 1986.)

One of the stories written by a pupil in the Leicester project, *Talking with Books* (1984) was presented in a **dual-language format** with drawings to illustrate the story (see Figure 24.1). Other formats such as **cartoon sequences** or **zig-zag** or **pull-out books** can be designed or **whole class books** put together with contributions from every pupil. It is not very difficult to produce a **play** in written form if the children use tape recording to assist them with **transcription**, since they generally find it easier to approach such a challenge by enacting their ideas first and writing them afterwards.

The aim in making a book for children from another country would be similar for writing for any audience, in that there is the

Semina and Elephant-
Once upon a time There was a girl
Who lived in a little town Her name
was Semina She Lived with her mother
　　　　　One day her mother had
a heart attack so Semina went
out Side Started to cry
　　　　　She Saw The Elephant
came to See Semina was Frightened and
She run away The elephant followed her
To her home The elephant Saw Semina's
mother he Started crying too Semina's said
　　　　　to elephant are you my Fraind
The elephant Said yes and They lived happily
　　　　after ever.

تمینہ اور ہاتھی

ایک دن کا ذکر ہے کہ ایک گاؤں میں ایک لڑکی رہتی تھی
اس کا نام تمینہ تھا وہ اپنی ماں کے ساتھ رہتی تھی
ایک دن اس کی ماں مر گئ تمینہ باہر چلی
گئ اور رونے لگی وہ جنگل کی طرف چلنے لگی اس نے ایک
ہاتھی دیکھا تمینہ ڈر گئ اور بھاگ گئ ہاتھی بھی اس کے
پیچھے چلنے لگا اس کے گھر میں جب ہاتھی نے اس کی ماں کو
دیکھا اور وہ بھی رونے لگا تمینہ سے کہا تم میرے دوست
ہو ہاتھی نے کہا ہاں پھر دونوں ہنسی خوشی رہنے لگے

Osma's Story   'Talking with Books'Project 1984

Figure 24.1

need to keep in mind the purpose of the communication and the likely interests of the reader. To that end it may be helpful to compile a list of questions which pupils need to bear in mind or to ask directly in their book. The idea of letter writing may provide a simple way into the writing of a book or may form a part of the book itself.

Idea 3. Making a Videotape

It does not take too much of an imaginative leap to contemplate making a videotape as a possible next step!

Idea 4. Other Ways of Fostering International Literacy

In addition to encouraging literacy development within the UK by, for example, teaching/**assisting adults with basic reading and writing, teaching children with literacy difficulties,** or **encouraging children to enjoy reading, language and foreign languages,** there may be an interest in contributing more directly to ILY.

Figure 24.1 Continued

Teachers may wish to enter into **correspondence with colleagues in other countries**, to **write articles**, for example for professional journals which are designed particularly for such exchanges, or simply to describe their ways of teaching reading and writing in English within the National Curriculum. It may be of interest to **share such ideas at local level** through meeting with colleagues at a UKRA local council meeting, or **write for information about local, regional or national events** or to **contribute to publications and conferences** at national level.

There are two thriving UKRA interest groups, working on Linguistics in Teacher Education and on Record Keeping. These topics include obvious connections with both the National Curriculum in English and the development of children's as well as teachers' appreciation and knowledge of how language works. UKRA links with schools librarians are also strengthening and support for their continued resourcing of schools is being sought, particularly for maintaining and developing the range of resources required for fostering interest in international as well as national development of literacy.

For information on any of the above topics or ways of linking with international contacts for ILY projects, please complete the following appended invitation form.

We trust that you will find this kind of involvement in sharing your work and extending your pupils' literacy development to be stimulating, professionally encouraging and helpful in a practical way. It is also a very cost effective way of becoming involved in contributing to the forum for exchange of information on reading and related matters and for making a contribution, should you wish, to collaborative research and development towards international literacy while celebrating literacy and International Literacy Year.

Appendix

Please feel free to photocopy, complete and send to: UKRA Office, Edgehill College, St Helen's Road, Ormskirk, Lancs. L39 4QP

Celebrating Literacy: Making International Links for ILY and the 1990s.
Invitation to Contribute to International Literacy through UKRA

Information for ILY Links

Name: ....

Early Years/Juniors/Primary/Special/
Librarian/Other (please specify)

....

School address: ....

School telephone: ....

Member of UKRA: Yes/No

I would like information on/an application for school membership/individual membership [please delete as appropriate].

I would like the following [please tick appropriate boxes].
1 Contact name and address for linking with a school or class in
  Country ....

  Preferred age range ....

2 Information about the European Committee □

3 Information about the International Reading Association □

4 Other ....

I am interested in links for ILY
(a) with a class within the UK but in another area □
(b) with a class in Europe □
(c) with a class in the USA □
(d) with a class in Australia □
(e) with a class in Japan □
(f) with a class in Hong Kong □
(g) with a class in [please state country] ....

Information for UKRA

1   I am interested in trying out the idea for audiotape links   ☐
2   I am interested in trying out ideas for making a book/video/other [please circle]
3   I am willing to send copies of the children's work for sharing with UKRA colleagues at the 1990 Annual Conference at Nottingham University in the last week of July

☐

4   I am willing to give/seek permission for the children's work/my written submission to be published in any UKRA professional report sharing responses to ILY   ☐

I already contribute to developing literacy by

teaching adults   ☐

teaching children with literacy difficulties (including, for example, specific learning difficulties, dyslexia, or other special needs in basic literacy – please state)..
....

encouraging children's love of literature, such as through Family Reading Groups

☐

I am willing to offer the following ideas for ILY [please state below or use a separate sheet]